S0-FQJ-008

THE PSYCHOLOGY OF
WESTERN CULTURE

The Psychology of
Western Culture

by
JOHN COLBY MYER

PHILOSOPHICAL LIBRARY
New York

Copyright 1972 by PHILOSOPHICAL LIBRARY INC.
15 East 40 Street, New York, N. Y. 10016

All rights reserved

Library of Congress Catalog Card No. 72-82791
SBN 8022-2096-7

Printed in the United States of America

DEDICATED TO MY WIFE,

MARTHA HAMBLIN

WHO GIVES ME UNFAILING
SUPPORT AND TO

ROBERT J. BERKLEY

WHO IS A SCHOLAR, BIBLIOPHILE,
CRITIC AND GOOD FRIEND

Table of Contents

LIST OF ILLUSTRATIONS

Plate Number 27: "Madonna of the Long Neck," Parmigianino, Uffizi.

Plate Number 28: "Presentation of the Virgin," Tintoretto, *Santa Maria dell'Orto*, Venice.

Plate Number 29: "Last Judgment," Michelangelo, *Sistine Chapel*, Vatican.

Plate Number 30: Detail from "Last Judgment," *Christ as Righteous Judge.*

Plate Number 31: "Baptism of Christ," El Greco, Prado, Madrid.

Plate Number 32: "Burial of Count Orgaz," El Greco, *St. Tome*, Toledo.

Plate Number 33: "Landscape with Burial of Phocion," Poussin, The Louvre.

Plate Number 34: "The Garden of Love," Rubens, Prado.

Plate Number 35: Photograph, *Colonnade in front of St. Peter's*, Bernini, Vatican.

Plate Number 36: "A Pilgrimage to Cytheria," Watteau, The Louvre.

Plate Number 37: "The Rake's Progress III," Hogarth, Sir John Soane's Museum, London.

Plate Number 38: "Marriage a la Mode," *Breakfast Scene*, Hogarth, National Gallery, London.

Plate Number 39: Four etchings from "The Capriccios," Goya, Prado. Original plate numbers 20, 23, 63 and 65.

Plate Number 40: Four etchings from "The Disasters of the War," Goya, Prado. Original plate numbers 15, 19, 43 and 72.

Plate Number 41: Photograph, *The Royal Pavilion at Brighton*, John Nash, 1818.

Plate Number 42: Photograph, *The Houses of Parliament*, London, Sir Charles Barry, designed 1835.

Plate Number 43: "Moulin de la Galette," Renoir, The Louvre, Paris.

Plate Number 44: "Dance at Bougival," Renoir, Museum of Fine Arts, Boston.

Plate Number 45: "Olympia," Manet, The Louvre.

Plate Number 46: "Venus of Urbino," Titian, Uffizi.

Plate Number 47: "Study of Rouen Cathedral—Early Morning," Monet, Museum of Fine Arts, Boston.

Plate Number 48: "Isle of the Dead," Bocklin, Metropolitan Museum of Art, New York.

Plate Number 49: "The Bride," Rosetti, Tate Gallery, London.

Plate Number 50: "The Night," Hodler, Kunstmuseum, Bern.

Plate Number 51: "Melancholy and Mystery of a Street," de Chirico. Collection of Stanley R. Resor, Greenwich, Conn.

Plate Number 52: "Hide and Seek," Techelitchew, Museum of Modern Art, New York.

CHAPTER I

The Son of Man Response

In January of 1920 the art world of Paris was treated to an exhibition which included a reproduction of the *Mona Lisa* upon whose enigmatic face a luxuriant moustache had been painted. Among the *objets d'art* were a toy monkey labeled *Portrait of Cezanne* and an inkpot entitled *Blessed Virgin.*

In the same year at Cologne an art show was held in a little courtyard, the only access to which being through a public toilet where visitors were greeted by a young girl wearing her first communion dress and reciting obscene poetry.

A show held in New York featured a porcelain urinal and a bicycle wheel.

This activity was the work of a literary-artistic group calling itself DADA, a meaningless word discovered one day by a member of the organization who opened a dictionary at random, closed his eyes and pointed. His finger landed on *dada* which meant "rocking horse."

Meaninglessness, nihilism, and cynicism, the fruits of frustration, disillusion, and despair, were the principal characteristics of the movement during its early days. Europe had been bled white, Armageddon had come and gone and vultures sat upon the corpse of civilization. All of the sacrifices of "The war to make the world safe for democracy" and "The war to end wars" seemed to have been in vain. There was nothing left but to tear down and start over again. Dissonance was high.

Today in psychology *consistency theory*[1] postulates that

when an individual's beliefs and his actions are inconsistent, when they do not logically go together and support each other, an uncomfortable condition exists which is called *dissonance* and this may disturb the person enough so that he will change either his belief or his actions in the direction of a more consistent and comfortable relationship between them.

We postulate that the same process operates for groups of people and that during certain periods of history dissonance is low; thinking and doing, faith and practice, ethos and style, tend to go together in a system of mutual support. There is a consistent form, pattern or configuration in the culture. We might even use the wonderful German word *Gestalt;* in a good Gestalt one finds a well-ordered, closed, and internally consistent framework of reference. It sounds safe and pleasant, but under such conditions enterprise may tend to stagnate and there will be little motivation for change. Artistic expression becomes formalized, manners are frozen in an encasing system of etiquette, and Government is safely in the hands of the POWERS THAT BE; of an "establishment." No one paints a moustache on the Mona Lisa; no one dares.

On the other hand there have been transitionary periods of change, times infused with restless questing when the newly emerging world of action is not consistent with the established belief system, when the powers of a *status quo* are inadequate to cope with the events of the day. In other words, periods of high dissonance which motivates and drives people. As a consequence one finds riots and revolutions, radical changes in the moral value system, brave new departures from convention in dress and manners, and an entirely new style of life.

We will be looking at buildings, paintings, poems, and even such objects as inkpots labeled "The Blessed Virgin" because they are readily available bits of evidence; observable behavioral responses made into the culture by the culture.

What is culture? We could use the word civilization and mean the same thing. Our concern is with all the products of the mind and hand of man which have emerged in the "West" and which constitute a common heritage for the majority of people living in Europe and the New World today.

We will look at human behavior in some of its more general aspects, not focusing on differences which exist among various religious and ethnic groups, but rather asking how things are the same; what properties a collection of objects and events have in common. For our purpose the collection will consist of value systems and cultural products; of things that people believe and things which they do.

The history of the West has been uniquely influenced by Christianity, and as the roots of Christianity lie in Judaism, a rather arbitrary start will be made with the Old Testament book of Daniel written shortly after 175 B.C. This was a time of crisis and heroic struggle when it seemed as if the little Jewish nation was doomed to final extinction. Traditionally we look to Greece for the origins of Western civilization; curiously enough in this situation Greeks were persecuting Jews. Not the heroic Greeks who had withstood the Persian invasions nor the beautiful Greeks of the Golden Age, but rather some of the heirs of that Alexander whom we call the Great, the one who had conquered the world. The idea of democracy was pretty well dead in the near eastern portion of Alexander's former empire when the King, a certain Antiochus Epiphanes, decided to stamp out the Jewish religion. A hero, Judas Maccabeus, appeared to drive out the enemy and establish the last Jewish state to exist until modern times. It was against this background of struggle and sacrifice that a prophet known as Daniel wrote:

> I saw in my vision by night, and behold, the four winds of heaven were stirring up the great sea. And four great beasts came up out of the sea . . . and (one of them) was lifted up from the ground and made to stand on two feet like a man; and the mind of a man was given to it . . . and behold, (I saw a) fourth beast, terrible and dreadful and exceeding strong; and it had great iron teeth; it devoured and broke in pieces, and stamped the residue with its feet.[2]

This is representative of writing which is known as apocryphal and apocalyptic. Apocrypha means hidden; the real meaning is cloaked in allegory so that only the reader with inside knowledge will understand that the ultimate Great Beast is Antiochus Ephipanes. It is also an apocalypse or prediction of ultimate last things; of the final days when God will vindicate Himself and bring the present evil world order to an end. Typically such writing is rich in visions, trances, and ecstasies and is produced during periods of troubled times. It is intended to impart strength and courage to people whose condition is so desperate that nothing but a faint hope seems to remain. It is darkest before the dawn, and surely the Lord God of Hosts will not desert His people; he *must* come soon now with great power to save and redeem. Daniel's vision continues with more bizarre horrors until he sees "the Ancient of Days" (God) seated on his throne and we have the famous messianic passage:

> And behold, with the clouds of heaven
> There came one like a SON OF MAN
> And he came to the Ancient of Days
> And was presented before him.
> And to him was given dominion
> And glory and kingdom,
> That all the peoples, nations and languages
> Should serve him;
> His dominion is an everlasting dominion
> Which shall not pass away,
> And his kingdom one
> That shall not be destroyed.[3]

For Daniel the Son of Man was a heavenly figure of supernatural power identified somehow with the nation and religion which he loved. Part of the "prophecy" did come true; the Syrian armies of the Greek king were beaten back and the Temple at Jerusalem was cleansed and rededicated. But other Great Beasts were lurking under the horizon of time waiting to stamp out, devour, destroy, and grind the residue under foot. In 63 B.C. Roman legions marched into Jerusalem.

For the next hundred years secret writings and revelations continued to pour out in great abundance. Some of them are included in that section of the Bible found between the Old and New Testaments known as *The Apocrypha*. For example the third chapter of *The Wisdom of Solomon,* starts with:

> But the souls of the righteous are in the hands of God, and there shall no torment touch them. In the sight of the unwise they shall seem to die: and their departure is taken for misery, and their going from us to be utter desolation: but they are in peace. For though they be punished in the sight of men, yet is their hope full of immortality. And having been chastised, they shall be greatly rewarded: for God proved them and found them worthy of himself. As gold in the furnace hath he tried them, and received them as a burnt offering. And in the time of their visitation they shall shine, and run to and fro like sparks among the stubble.[4]

This was written about the year 40 A.D. by a Greek-speaking Jew in the city of Alexandria. The use of the name Solomon was a literary device to lend authority to the writing in the same way that many of the Psalms of David were written long after David's time by people who chose to remain anonymous. Whoever he was, this particular person was addressing himself to the large colony of Jews in Alexandria, people who had fled from "bondage" in the homeland, a sort of Exodus in reverse. In Egypt the universal language was Greek, and some of the migrated Jews were forgetting Hebrew, so they must be reached in the language which they understood. There were persecutions in Alexandria as well as in Jerusalem, and in the face of this our unknown author offers the hope of immortality; the souls of the righteous are in the hands of God.

Presently the newly emerging sect of Christians were included with Jews as targets for persecution and became the chief scapegoat in Nero's Rome of 64 A.D. The following year we find John Mark writing:

> But on those days, after that tribulation, the sun will be darkened, and the moon will not give its light, and

5

the stars will be falling from heaven, and the powers of the heavens will be shaken. And then they will see the SON OF MAN coming in clouds with great power and glory. And then he will send out his angels and gather his elect from the four winds, from the ends of the earth to the ends of heaven.[5]

In Mark's Gospel one senses great haste and urgency. In the eyes of many the group of peculiar people for whom he was writing belonged to a sort of lunatic fringe; they believed that God's special agent, the SON OF MAN, had *already* visited them under a disguise to scout out the situation, and that NOW, perhaps even tonight, he would return in the clouds of heaven, revealing his true identity in great power and glory.

As Christians went to their deaths singing hymns and looking toward heaven, a group of desperate Jews rose in open rebellion. One of their leaders, Josephus, organized an "army" which went forth to meet the Roman legions under Vespasian and Titus. The Jewish forces broke and fled, Titus laid seige to Jerusalem and after untold misery the Holy City fell and the Temple was destroyed once more.

At the time of the seige a Christian known to us as Saint Luke wrote in his Gospel:

> When you see Jerusalem surrounded by armies, then know that its desolation is come near. . . . And there will be signs in the sun and the moon and stars, and upon the earth distress of nations in perplexity at the roaring of the sea and the waves, men fainting with fear and foreboding at what is coming on the world: . . . And then they will see the SON OF MAN coming in a cloud with power and great glory. Now when these things begin to take place, look up and raise your heads, because your redemption is drawing near.[6]

About twenty-five years later, in 95 A.D., came the severe persecutions under Domitian. At this time we find the writer of the Book of Revelation saying:

Then I turned to see the voice that was speaking to me, and on turning I saw seven golden lampstands, and in the midst of the lampstands one like a SON OF MAN, clothed with a long robe and a golden girdle about his breast; . . . from his mouth issued a sharp two-edged sword, and his face was like the sun shining in full strength.[7]

During the quarter century since the writings of Mark and Luke some changes had taken place in the popular expectation regarding the imminence of the second coming in power and glory. The SON OF MAN is now seen as fairly well fixed in heaven and perhaps we will have to go to him rather than wait for him to come down to us. It was believed that the surest, shortest way to him was by way of martyrdom. Many went to their deaths in a transport of mystical ecstasy. The writer of *Revelation* says of them:

These are they who have come out of great tribulation; they have washed their robes and made them white in the blood of the Lamb. Therefore they are before the throne of God. . . . For the Lamb in the midst of the throne will be their shepherd, and he will guide them to springs of living water; and God will wipe away every tear from their eyes.[8]

Some fifteen or twenty years after this was written a strange company of people wound its way from Antioch in Syria to Rome. There were ten soldiers and their prisoner, Ignatius, the bishop of Antioch, who had been condemned to be thrown to the lions in the Coliseum. Although under heavy guard, he speaks of "being bound to ten leopards, that is, a squad of soldiers, who get worse the better they are treated,"[9] yet on the journey Ignatius is able to write several long letters and to receive delegations from various Christian communities along the way. He is anxious that there be no rescue operation to deprive him of his opportunity for final witness and martyrdom. In a letter which he sent on ahead to the Christians at Rome he says:

7

May I enjoy the wild beasts that are prepared for me, and I pray that I may find them quick. I will coax them to devour me quickly, not as in the case of some whom they were afraid to touch. If they will not of their own accord, I will force them to. Pardon me, I know what is best for me. I am just beginning to be a disciple. May nothing, visible or invisible stop my reaching the presence of Jesus Christ. Fire and cross and struggles with wild beasts, crushing of bones, mangling of limbs, grinding of my whole body, wicked torments of the devil, let them come upon me, only let me reach the presence of Jesus Christ.[10]

It did not take people long to elaborate accounts of martyrdom with stories of signs and wonders. Polycarp, bishop of Smyrna and friend of Ignatius, was put to death in 156 A.D. at the age of eighty-six. Shortly afterward a letter was written and circulated among the churches of Asia Minor. It gives a vivid description of attempts to burn the saint to death. The fire would not touch his body but "assumed an overreaching shape, like the sail of a ship filled by wind," the body glowed like silver or gold in a furnace and the witnesses "perceived such a fragrance as a breath of incense or some other precious spice."[11] Presently the executioner was ordered to go up and stab the body with a dagger, whereupon a dove emerged from the wound and such a great quantity of blood that the fire was put out.*

This is perhaps the first in a long line of miracle stories which found their way into *Lives of the Saints* and *Books of Martyrs*.

There is a large body of literature attributed to various personages of the New Testament where the authorship is obviously spurious. Montague Rhodes James in his scholarly work *The Apocryphal New Testament*[12] lists seven Gospels, a dozen narratives about the infancy and childhood of Jesus, and the collected correspondence of such worthies as Pontius Pilate, Joseph of Arimathea, Nicodemus, and many more.

---

* Could any of this imagery have derived from *The Wisdom of Solomon* quoted on p. 5: "As gold in the furnace hath he tried them. . . ."

The general theme is the miraculous intervention of supernatural beings into human existence.

Here is a major component of the belief system which was to dominate Europe for the next twelve hundred years or more. In essence it was dualistic; man was both a physical and a spiritual being who labored here in the world below but whose reward was in heaven and the reward was nothing less than the resurrection of the body and the life everlasting. There were very definite and real connections between the two worlds and frequent traffic between them. Thinking was completely non-rational; trees could talk, stones bleed, people fly through the air, and the sun could stop and dance in the sky. Angels and demons were everywhere and popular religion was more oriented toward magic than toward ethical monotheism. The Son of Man, who once had been an allegorical figure symbolizing the ultimate and inscrutable purpose of God, successively became a Person who lived a human life, then a heavenly figure poised and ready to swoop down to earth at any moment, then the second person of the Holy Trinity who in some mysterious fashion was also the "Lamb in the midst of the throne."

This sort of writing, particularly the apocalyptic visions of Daniel and the "pure" Son of Man response, is most frequently found during periods of troubled times marked by catastrophic warfare, persecutions, massacres, and hopeless misery. This is most likely to come from the pen of a mystic who operates outside the sphere of ordinary reason and logic. One finds a great surging up of subconscious material which emerges before the inner vision as a great light; as a conversion experience or revelation. These are the visions of the earliest and formative years of a belief system. They are quite different from the *Moustache on the Mona Lisa* type response which occurs at a time of disillusion and cynicism when a belief system is falling apart. When belief is new, exciting and a bit dangerous, before it has become a *system,* we find the greatest proliferation of wonder stories.

For example, the Angel Gabriel appears to Mary and says to her "Hail, thou that art highly favored, the Lord is with thee: blessed art thou among women."[13] On the road to Damascus, Saul is struck by a great light and emerges as Paul the Apostle. More recently, the angel Moroni appeared to Joseph Smith in Vermont and the Latter Day Saints came into existence.

Today we observe the phenomenon of a "drug culture" or "hippie sub-culture" which is actively engaged in seeking revelations and mystical experiences by way of LSD, systematic exercises in meditation, witchcraft and whatever. There is a brisk revival of such non-rational activities as the operation of a Ouija board, consulting Tarot cards, or having one's horoscope cast by an astrologer. The Magus, Swami, and Guru are coming into their own as father figures; so far there seems to be a dearth of their counterparts among the ladies; perhaps the new feminism will produce a line of high priestesses and witch queens.

These newly emerging beliefs are in a very early stage of formation and as yet there is no new belief *system;* people are simply groping about subconsciously seeking to reduce the high dissonance of this generation. The problem is to find a system of values which is compatible with chaotic and irrational conditions of existence; perhaps all that we can say is that irrational belief is consistent with irrational behavior.

Let us return to the pages of history and see whether we can pick up any hints as to what to expect next. Christian faith and belief became Christian doctrine and dogma, complete with a hierarchical structure in heaven which was, in some fashion, isomorphic with the structure of society here on earth. At the apex of the heavenly structure was the Trinity containing within itself the mechanism of intercession as expressed in the Bible: ". . . We have an advocate with the Father, Jesus Christ the righteous: . . ."[14] However, a need was felt for additional steps in approaching the Apex and before long the role of Mary, the mother of the Lord, was expanded to perform this function. Many of these tales and legends were brought together in a Greek narrative of the seventh century and published under the name of St. John the Divine. Here are some excerpts:[15]

When as the all-holy and ever-virgin Mary, according to her custom went unto the holy sepulchre of our Lord to burn incense, and bowed her holy knees, she besought Christ our God that was born of her to come and abide with her. . . .

Now on one day which was Friday, the holy Mary came as she was wont to the sepulchre, and as she prayed it came to pass that the heavens were opend and the Archangel Gabriel came down to her. . . .

(Mary returns home and prays)

. . . and as she prayed, I, John came unto her, for the Holy Ghost caught me up by a cloud from Ephesus and set me in the place where the mother of my Lord lay. . . .

(presently the other apostles arrive on clouds, each gives a short account of his journey, then Mary prays again and)

After the prayer she said unto the apostles: cast on incense and pray. And when they had prayed there came a thunder from heaven and a terrible sound as of chariots, and lo, a multitude of the host of angels and powers, and a voice as the SON OF MAN was heard, and the Seraphim came 'round the house wherein the holy and spotless mother of God, the virgin, lay: . . .

(there follow various signs and wonders, then Christ arrives:)

And as we all prayed there appeared innumerable multitudes of angels, and the Lord riding upon the Cherubim in great power . . . and the Lord abode with her, saying: Behold, henceforth shall thy precious body be translated into paradise, and thy holy soul shall be in the heavens in the treasuries of my Father in surpassing brightness . . .

(next follows the commission giving Mary the power of surrogate and chief intercessor, *almost* co-equal with her Son . . .)

11

The Lord said to his own mother: Let thine heart be glad and rejoice; for every grace and every gift hath been given thee of my Father which is in heaven and of me and of the Holy Ghost. EVERY SOUL THAT CALLETH UPON THY NAME . . . SHALL FIND MERCY AND CONSOLATION AND SUCCOR AND CONFIDENCE, BOTH IN THIS WORLD AND THAT WHICH IS TO COME.

This story became a very popular belief and was the subject matter for many paintings. See Plate No. 1 which illustrates the following passage from the text:[16]

. . . and the Lord spread forth his unstained hands and received her holy and spotless soul. And at the going forth of her spotless soul the place was filled with sweet odour and light unspeakable, and lo, a voice from heaven was heard, saying: Blessed art thou among women.

There is meticulous attention to the details of the story in this painting. The unknown artist is using Gothic magic realism; realistic techniques to illustrate an imaginary event. At first glance the little central figure seems to be that of an infant, but on *second* glance we find that it is an exact miniature of Mary appropriately vested as Queen of Heaven.

In attempting to trace this legend one is led back to Jewish and early Christian apocalyptic and perhaps even to Babylonian mythology. In the Book of Revelation we read:

And there appeared a great wonder in heaven; a woman clothed with the sun, and the moon under her feet, and upon her head a crown of twelve stars: and she being great with child cried, travailing in birth, and pained to be delivered. . . . And she brought forth a man child, who was to rule all nations with a rod of iron: and her child was caught up unto God, and to his throne.[17]

This was written some five hundred years before the above quoted Greek narrative of the assumption of the Virgin, and the imagery here derives from still older sources. The figure of the woman in heaven may have originally been that of a moon goddess, crowned with the twelve signs of the zodiac, who gave birth to Marduk, the sun god. The writer of Revelation seems to apply the figure of the woman to the church and he goes on to describe struggles against the powers of evil and persecution from which the church will emerge victorious. Perhaps now the twelve stars in her crown are the twelve apostles. Then there is a gradual reinterpretation to fit the needs of the times and the woman becomes the Blessed Virgin. This is at a considerable remove from the DADA exhibition of an inkwell labeled "Blessed Virgin."*

Two attributes of divinity, starting life on earth with a miraculous birth and ending it with an ascension into heaven, were ascribed to the SON OF MAN by the early New Testament writers. With the passage of time these attributes are also ascribed to the Mother of God; none of this material is found in the Bible. The biblical story of the Virgin Birth refers to Jesus having been born of a virgin; the subsequent story of the Immaculate Conception carries the phenomenon back a generation and refers to the conception of Mary; that is *her* mother St. Ann did not conceive her by an earthly father. Again the early belief in the ascension of the resurrected body of Jesus finds its counterpart in the later belief in the assumption or bodily taking to heaven of Mary who emerges as the all-encompassing Mother.

Feminism is not new, we all have heard of "Mother Nature" and "Mother Earth"; some of us have heard of "Our Holy Mother the Church." The female principle, lacking in Judaism, occupied a prominent place in contemporary pagan religions. In *The Divine Passion* Vardis Fisher describes the ecstasies of mating between a pagan priest and priestess; he says:

> And she was Malkath, the Mother-goddess, who was Ishtar who was Ashtoreth who was Astarte. She was Dimiter, goddess of earth and corn, who mated with the Sky; she was Hera, who mingled in love with Zeus; she

---
* See p. 1.

was Artemis the many breasted, she was Aphrodite, she was Venus. . . . She was Cybele whose temple stood on the high places and whose music was cymbals; and she was Isis the bride of Osiris, and so intimate was the union of Earth and Sun that she was his wife and his sister and he was her husband and her brother . . . and she would be Sin the moon-god. She had been the moon and now she was the earth, and she would be the Queen of Heaven and the Mother of God.[18]

During New Testament times there was a confusion of idioms; the Son of David became the Son of Man who was the Good Shepherd, the Lamb in the midst of the throne and *also* the Bridegroom with the figure of the Bride representing the Church. As late as 1866 it was possible to write:

> From heaven he came and sought her
> To be his holy bride;
> With his own blood he bought her,
> And for her life he died.[19]

In Christianity the female principle is incarnate in both Mary and the Church; in both Mother and Bride. One thinks of a large scale Oedipus complex. The Old Testament father figure had been too strict.

During the middle ages God the Father was seen as playing a rather vague and peripheral role. God the Son, while still available, would be best approached by way of His Mother. The original SON OF MAN response has changed with changing times and conditions and we find it replaced by the cult of saints and the cult of relics which will be discussed further on. But a SON OF MAN type response continues to be emitted when the stimulus conditions are heavily charged with fear, anxiety, misery, and frustration. Negro spirituals are a case in point. It was people in bondage who sang: "Swing low, sweet chariot, comin' fo to carry me home."

REFERENCES

1. L. Festinger, *A Theory of Cognitive Dissonance* (Stanford: Stanford University Press, 1957).
2. *The Bible* (King James Version—KJV) Daniel, 7:2-7.
3. *The Bible* (Revised Standard Version—RSV) Daniel, 7:13-14.
4. *The Apocrypha*, KJV Wisdom of Solomon, 3:1-7.
5. *The Bible*—KJV Mark, 13:24-27.
6. *The Bible*—RSV Luke, 21:20, 25-28.
7. *Ibid.*, Revelation, 1:12-13, 16.
8. *Ibid.*, Revelation, 7:14-15, 17.
9. E. J. Goodspeed (ed.), *The Apostolic Fathers* (New York: Harper, 1950), pp. 222-223. The letter of Ignatius to the Romans, 5:1.
10. *Ibid.*, 5:2-3.
11. *Ibid.*, pp. 247-256. The Martyrdom of Polycarp.
12. M. R. James (ed.), *The Apocryphal New Testament* (Oxford: Oxford University Press, 1924).
13. *The Bible*—KJV, *op. cit.*, Luke, 1:28.
14. *Ibid.*, I John, 2:1-2.
15. James, *op. cit.*, Greek Narrative, p. 207.
16. *Ibid.*, p. 208.
17. *The Bible, op. cit.*, Revelation, 12:1-2, 5.
18. V. Fisher, *The Divine Passion* (Pyramid Books Edition, 1961), pp. 287-288.
19. S. S. Wesley, The Hymnal of the Protestant Episcopal Church, 1940. Hymn No. 396.

CHAPTER II

Martyrs and Heretics

Early in the Civil War Julia Ward Howe, while doing a turn through Northern army camps, heard a group of soldiers singing:

> John Brown's body lies a mould'ring in the ground,
> John Brown's body lies a mould'ring in the ground,
> John Brown's body lies a mould'ring in the ground,
> But his soul goes marching on.
>
> Glory, glory, Hallelujah!
> Glory, glory, Hallelujah!
> Glory, glory, Hallelujah!
> His soul goes marching on.

After she got home Mrs. Howe wrote the words of "The Battle Hymn of the Republic" to the tune she had heard. (Mine eyes have seen the glory of the coming of the Lord, etc.) This was heady stuff and served to keep up the morale of the tired and discouraged troops during some of the darker days of the war.

Frequently the soldiers would insert a verse or two of "John Brown's Body" into the "Battle Hymn." John Brown was a martyr. He had led the raid on Harpers Ferry in 1859, where some people maintain the first shots of the Civil War were fired, and for his pains was captured, tried, and hung by the neck until dead. Incidentally, the officer in charge of the execution was Major Thomas Jonathan Jackson, U.S.A., later to become "Stonewall" Jackson, C.S.A.

The list of martyrs is a long one. It includes those who, like Ignatius* volunteered their bodies as a sacrifice, as well as those who would have preferred another fate such as a young man today who "gives his life for his country" when he may not be at all sympathetic with what his country is fighting for.

Some martyrs have gradually been forgotten; others live on in the minds of those who hold their memories in reverence. For a while King Charles the First became "Blessed Charles the Martyr," coming as close to canonization as is possible in the Church of England; today his image is not widely venerated. Horst Wessel, a young man killed in a street brawl, lent his name to the official song of the Nazi party; today he is happily forgotten. John Birch, a young American Air Force captain who was killed in 1945, has lent his name to a Society which many of us wish might be forgotten. Could we predict that someday there will be songs or societies dedicated to an Angela Davis or a Doctor Spock?

There is a wide gulf between the fact of martyrdom and the need which people have for a martyr. The circumstances of martyrdom differ but the need is universal. Perhaps we can say that there is need for an ambiguous object to which people can project and with which they can identify; a symbol, a figure, the personification of an ideal, someone whom they do not know personally, someone who does not whine at them and whose screams they have never heard. John Brown's body may be a mould'ring in the ground but we do not want to see the body or smell the rot; all we want to do is sing about it. When it is too close to home it gets sticky; I do not want Mother to work her fingers to the bone for me, especially if she frequently shows me her bleeding fingers.

The Martyr is not quite the same as the Hero whose image is exalted during times of achievement; rather it is a figure needed during times leading up to achievement or during

---

* See pp. 7-8, Chapter I.

times when the SON OF MAN response is being made, the figure of one who will bear our griefs and sorrows, of one who has withstood persecution and been rejected for some great CAUSE.

In Judaism there is the suggestion that redemption is wrought through suffering. A prophet known as "Second Isaiah" wrote:

> He is despised and rejected of men; a man of sorrows and acquainted with grief: and we hid as it were our faces from him; he was despised, and we esteemed him not. Surely he hath borne our griefs, and carried our sorrows.[1]

This is one of the "suffering servant" passages from Isaiah which presents a messianic figure quite different from Daniel's "son of man." Isaiah's servant is a prototype martyr and the "servant" was one of the roles ascribed to the Christ. We have the persecuted one who also came in grandeur, glory, and great power. It sounds almost paranoid. This is a phenomenon almost unique to Western culture. Buddha departed into a never-never land of nothingness; Mohammed ascended to a paradise of carnal delights; Hercules and Sigfried were heroes. Only in Christendom has God fulfilled the role of suffering servant and it is in the West that people find the greatest need for martyrs.

We have been looking at the evolution of a belief system and sooner or later we must expect to find something labeled "wrong belief," and this, of course, is heresy. We do not have long to wait. Not more than twenty years after the Crucifixion St. Paul wrote to the Galatians: "As we said before, so say I again, if any man preach any other gospel unto you than that ye have received, let him be accursed."[2] In his first epistle to Timothy, Paul mentions two by name who have made a shipwreck of faith: "Of whom is Hymenaeus and Alexander; whom I have delivered unto Satan, that they may learn not to blaspheme."[3] One wonders what *delivering unto Satan* consisted of. Perhaps some sort of curse or primitive excommunication. The New Testament abounds in references to "false prophets."

19

Like a traveler at night in a strange country treading his way between swamps and pitfalls, the early church maneuvered around various heresies. An early contender was *Gnosticism* which was actually a diffuse trend parallel to the prevalent mystery cult religions. A Gnostic was one with special, hidden, "higher" knowledge; one who was an adept with revealed, esoteric gnosis. Christian Gnosticism tended to reduce God to a philosophical abstraction and to regard Jesus as the vehicle for the divine spirit which had entered his body at his baptism and departed before the crucifixion. It was impossible that the divine Logos could have hung upon a cross and suffered. The role of suffering servant was out.

During New Testament times St. Paul refers despairingly to Gnosticism which he calls "the wisdom of the Greeks" and "philosophy." He wrote to the Colossians: "As ye have therefore received Christ Jesus the Lord, so walk ye in him: rooted and built up in him, and established in the faith, as ye have been taught, . . . Beware lest any man spoil you with philosophy. . . . Let no man therefore judge you in meat, or in drink, or in respect of a holiday, or the new moon, or of the sabbath days."[4] The Gnostics at Collosae were teaching the elaborate rituals of a mystery religion in which the initiates were expected to follow special diets, observe a variety of holidays and fast days, and perform many sacramental acts of purification. The trend was in the direction of theosophy heavily larded with mysticism; had Christianity developed in this direction it would have become a sort of superordinate secret society excluding the common man, the man whom St. Paul was so anxious to include.

Another major heresy was Arianism, named after Arius (256-336), a priest of the diocese of Alexandria in Egypt. This was a phase in the long, drawn out controversy over the nature of Christ. Some tended toward the Gnostic point of view that God was utterly transcendent and unaccessible and that the Son was unlike the Father; others believed that the Son was "of like substance with the Father"; others compromised and said that he was similar to the Father. Arius refused to compromise and pushed the Gnostic viewpoint to its logical conclusion; the nature of Christ was completely divine; he did not have a human soul; the son of man was not a servant, he was mystical, transcendent, other and holy. This tended to reduce dissonance by solving the paradox of a double nature. Arianism was consistent at one end of a spectrum in the same way that today Unitarianism is consistent at the other end, the end which completely denies any divine nature. There is a certain appeal to either extreme, the appeal of consistency, logic, and low dissonance, but Christian orthodoxy was to hammer out its position in the middle, in the area of the paradox. Orthodoxy is something that must be built up over a period of time and, as in the development of a legal code, cases must be tried and examined to form a body of opinion. If you win the contest you are right and if you lose you are wrong, or in theological terms, a heretic.

Martyrs and heretics coexisted during the early days of the church. The age of persecution which produced martyrs was the same age in which the church wrestled with the problem of true belief. Ignatius, Polycarp, and thousands of others did not die for some vague ideal but for something much more concrete, something more definite, for a credo which could be identified and spelled out. Obviously someone who died for a wrong belief died in vain.

In the year 313 the Edict of Milan legalized Christianity and presently the Emperor, Constantine, became a Christian and was no longer a reasonable candidate for the role of apocalyptic Great Beast. This must have required considerable intellectual gymnastics because a few short years before the Christians had suffered their worst persecution under Constantine's predecessor Diocletian. The stupendous ruins of the baths of Diocletian can still be seen in Rome. When completed, during the height of the persecution, they were among the most outstanding public buildings of the city, able to accommodate more than three thousand patrons at one time. They were the last word in sumptuous magnificence where every whim of a wealthy client could be satisfied by the army of slaves who scurried through cleverly constructed underground passageways fetching and carrying oil, food, books, towels, and other requirements. Evidently many of these slaves were Christians, members of the disenfranchised, persecuted minority, who quite naturally associated both the luxury of the baths and the horrors of persecution with the Emperor.

But the new emperor was becoming a Christian, and presently many of the patrons of the baths became Christians. One could even find clergy who bathed and anointed their beards with scented oil. Here was a dissonance producing paradox of a major order.

And to add to the confusion at this time the Arian controversy was in full swing. This "heresy" dominated most of North Africa and the East and one of Constantine's sons became converted to this way of thinking. Clearly if the new emperor were to use his new religion as an effective political force the church must be strong and united, so to this end he called a general council at Nicea in the year 325.

The bishops duly met and argued, chiefly over Arianism, until Constantine intervened and made a few key decisions effecting a compromise out of which emerged most of the Nicene creed as we know it today. In this Jesus Christ is described as "being of one substance with the Father," that is, completely God, and at the same time he "was incarnate by the Holy Ghost of the Virgin Mary, and was made man." In other words he was *also* completely human.

It took many years to consolidate the powerful structure which became the Medieval Papacy. In 381 another council convened at Constantinople to more clearly define the role of the Holy Ghost; in 431 the council of Ephesus further defined the position of the Virgin Mary; twenty years later at Chalcedon an instrument was forged defining the two natures of Christ in greater detail. Four more great Ecumenical Councils of the "undivided" Church were held prior to the permanent split between East and West in the year 1054. Heresy became progressively more easy to detect as orthodoxy became more clearly defined.

We have been considering, as a specific case, the development of Christianity, but this inevitably brings us to relation-

Plate Number 1: "Falling Asleep of the Blessed Virgin", Bohemian. 14th cent. Museum of Fine Arts, Boston.

Plate Number 2: "The Temptation of St. Anthony", Bosch. National Museum, Lisbon.

Plate Number 3: "St. Jerome at Prayer", Bosch. Museum of Fine Arts, Ghent.

Plate Number 4: Photograph, *Mausoleum of Galla Placidia*, Ravenna.

Plate Number 5: Photograph, *Interior of St. Apollinaire Nuovo,* Ravenna.

Plate Number 6:   Mosaic, "The Last Supper" from St. Apollinaire
Nuovo, Ravenna.

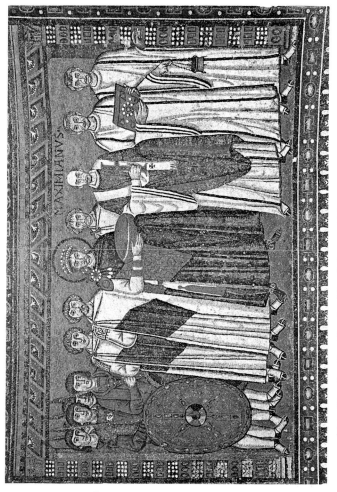

Plate Number 7: Mosaic, "Justinian and his Suite", St. Vitale, Ravenna.

Plate Number 8: Mosaic, "Theodora and her Suite", St. Vitale, Ravenna.

Plate Number 9: Photograph of wood carving, "A Dragon's Head" circa 820, Oslo University Museum.

Plate Number 10: Illuminated manuscript, title page of the *Book of Kells*, Trinity College, Dublin.

Plate Number 11: Tapestry, "The Battle of Hastings" from the *Bayeux Tapestry*, Bayeux, France.

Plate Number 12: Photograph, Notre-Dame de Paris, Paris

Plate Number 13: "Virgin and Child", Florentine, 13th cent. Uffizi.

Plate Number 14: "Virgin and Child", Duccio, Uffizi.

Plate Number 15: "Virgin and Child", Cimabue, Uffizi.

Plate Number 16: "Madonna Enthroned", Giotto, Uffizi.

ships between "church" and "state." Few will deny that Constantine's primary motive in espousing Christianity was to give an eleventh hour shot in the arm to the dying Colossus which was Rome; up to a point he was successful. He had gotten away with telling the bishops what to do and in the East this tended to continue where the authority of Patriarch and Emperor blended into a system of Caesaro-Papism, ultimately to flower in the vast Northern reaches of Holy Mother Russia. The last Nicholas was an intensely patriotic Slavophile, neither lazy, corrupt, nor self-seeking, completely dedicated to the mission which he was inadequate to perform. To him, his monarchy and his Russia were indeed Holy. Speaking of martyrs, it seems most improbable, but someday in the future July 16th may be a Holy Day dedicated to "The Martyrs of Ekateringburg" and people will remember the names of Nicholas, Alexandra, Olga, Tatinia, Marie, Anastasia, and Alexis. On July 16th, 1918, the Czar and his entire family were shot to death in the cellar of a little house in Ekateringburg, Siberia.

The quirks of fate are curious. The circumstances of martyrdom are quite similar; the chief difference between Ignatius, the early martyr, and Nicholas, the late martyr, lies in the fact that the former was on the side which ultimately won while the latter was on the side which lost.

Today when one says "church and state" various images come to mind. Perhaps it may be the gentle rustle of billowing white lawn sleeves as the bishops take their seats in the House of Lords or the memory of that dramatic moment when the Right Honorable and Most Reverend Geoffery Francis Fisher, ninety-ninth Archbishop of Canterbury and Primate of all England, placed the Crown of Saint Edward upon the head of Elizabeth, by the Grace of God Queen of England.

In a different context, one may think of Chinese sailors lining the deck of their ship and reciting in unison from the writings of Mao Tse-tung, holding their little red books with the same reverence which a pious Christian might show for his Bible. The little red book contains a gospel which indeed inspired devotion, a faith for which people will die and a religion which is very much part of the state. Articles of faith have been formalized into a creed which is explicit enough so that heretics can be easily detected. One hears that heresy in this situation can be a very uncomfortable condition.

Lenin digested a creed from the writings of Marx and Engels and made it official. Neither Lenin nor Stalin used the word "church" in connection with the new religion because it was completely indistinguishable from the state and this, of course, made heresy the same as treason. Might one speak of Stalin's purge victims as "martyrs?" At the time they were on the losing side, but the grains of sand are shifting in the hour glass of time and Stalin's body has been taken out of the reliquary on Red Square. No one knows where he lies buried.

Recall that when the old Church which had supported Louis XVI went down the drain with the blood spurting from the stump of His Majesty's severed neck, the New Order promptly changed the names of the months, inaugurating a new calendar starting with the YEAR ONE, and enthroned the Goddess of Reason in the cathedral of Notre Dame. People who persisted in "wrong belief" went to the guillotine.

Any kind of "church" represents belief in action, and the level of dissonance generated from this interaction is a function of whatever inconsistencies exist between the belief of an Ignatius or a Polycarp and the action of their martyrdom. But forced martyrdom is persecution, and there are inconsistencies between belief in a compassionate God of love and the horrible work of Torquemanda, the inquisitor general of Spain; between an act of assassination and belief in a new world of liberty and tolerance; between belief in the Prince of Peace and the act of war. Dissonance increases when the martyr does not go voluntarily to his death; when the heretic has martyrdom forced upon him.

REFERENCES

1. *The Bible*—KJV, Isaiah, 53:3-4.
2. *Ibid.*, Galatians, 1:9.
3. *Ibid.*, I Timothy, 1:20.
4. *Ibid.*, Colossians, 2:6-8, 16.

24

CHAPTER III

The Anti-Satan Response

It is no accident of history that the rise of monasticism during the fourth century coincided with the end of persecution. The great martyrs of the faith had lived and died during those first three centuries, they had fought the good fight, but now that Rome, the Great Beast, was becoming a Christian state, where was the enemy?

To some pure, zealous, and tough-minded Christians, Satan had gone underground and now lurked in pots of rouge, jugs of wine, and perfumed boudoirs. Temptations of the world and the lusts of the flesh were now becoming the principle activities of the Devil. Clearly a place like the baths of Diocletian was a temple of the dark God, a place steeped in sin and iniquity.

Saint Anthony of Egypt (about 250-355) is given credit for being the first Christian monk. Disgusted with the flesh-pots of Alexandria, he withdrew to the desert to practice the ascetic life and enter into combat with the hosts of evil. It is accounted that the Devil appeared to him under various guises, providing later generations with subject matter for the many "Temptation of St. Anthony" paintings to be found in our art galleries today.

Two such paintings hang in the Prado in Madrid and a third in the National Museum of Lisbon; they are from the brush of that mystical genius of surrealist fantasy, Hieronymus Bosch. We see violence turned inward upon the self; the torture of the mind; the anguished spirit living in a grotesque world from which all reason and value have departed. We see spiritual uncertainty, anxiety, tension, and dissonance. Here is visionary experience and revelation of the evil lying within the human personality. This is the discovery of sin and of the reality of damnation. (Plate No. 2)

We have no paintings or first-hand descriptions of St. Anthony any more than we have of the Virgin Mary. With Bosch, as with the Gothic painting of the death of Mary (see Plate No. 1) we are looking at an imaginative production created long after the event. The painting by Bosch, as are all other paintings, is a *response* which reflects, in part, the painter's own personality and, in part, the conditions of his existence. The cultural product emerges from the Zeitgeist and also helps create it. Bosch lived at the very end of the middle ages and St. Anthony shortly before the beginning of the dark ages. Their lives were separated by more than one thousand years. Yet there are certain common threads which begin with Anthony and end with Bosch; there is a continuity of paradox which will be looked at in more detail later on in chapters four and five. Briefly it is the paradox of dualism, of sinful, suffering humanity living here in the real world of Satan and his minions, while the higher reality, the ultimate upper road, was the path which led to heaven and the beatific vision. Losing sight of this vision produced the horrible sensation of GUILT.

The response to the agony of guilt is self-punishment; one's own robes must be washed and made white in one's own blood, sweat, and tears. Man must justify himself before God, which is a completely different thing from God vindicating himself before his Chosen People. In the SON OF MAN response we get the impression that God has let his people down and ultimately He must feel obliged to swoop down with great redemptive power. In the ANTI-SATAN response man is seen as having let God down; man wallows in sin and filth, and the only road back is by way of heroic exercises in self purification. Now the war is against temptation, the new heroes of the faith are those who are able to drag themselves out of the

26

cesspool of iniquity which is the WORLD, and the arena of combat is not the Coliseum, but the human psyche.

Saint Jerome (about 347-420) was such a hero. He led a restless life of retreats to the desert, visits to monastic centers, and pilgrimages to the Holy Land. Like so many others before and since, he had an intense mystical experience as a young man, a vision in which he was summoned before a court of divine justice and severely punished for spending too much time in the study of classic literature to the exclusion of his Christian vocation. He promptly departed for the desert to become a hermit and atone for his sin by fasting, meditation, and prayer. Bosch has painted a powerful picture of this; *St. Jerome at Prayer*, which now hangs in the Musee des Beaux-Arts at Ghent. (Plate No. 3)

Jerome displays the most intense concentration. His facial expression and bodily attitude remind one of a patient in the schizophrenic ward of a mental hospital. He is surrounded by weird and other-worldly objects which experts tell us are the occult symbols of heresy. To a psychologist they look like the furnishings of an interior, private world of fantasy.

Look at the complete split between the softly lit distance, which seems like a bit of the real world, and the ominously shadowy foreground constructed out of dead and dying organic matter. Directly in front of the saint is an egg-like object sprouting whiskers and bathed in the phosphorescent glow of putresence.

In this painting all action is arrested; we are looking at a frozen moment in introspective agony.

Unlike Anthony, however, Jerome did not spend the rest of his life in the desert. His need for other people was apparently too great, and soon we find him wandering about again, preaching personal holiness, self-denial, and, above all, virginity. He was the chief exponent of the doctrine that Mary remained a virgin throughout her entire lifetime; that the people described in the New Testament as the "Lord's brothers" must have been cousins or some other relation; it was unthinkable that the Mother of God should ever have conceived in a normal (i.e. sinful) manner. We may assume that

27

stories about the assumption of the Virgin discussed in Chapter I were originating at about this time.

Jerome was continually surrounded by pious women; widows and virgins whom he instructed in the spiritual life. Another interesting facet of his character was scholarship of a rather high order. He did a vast amount of translating, editing, and commenting on Holy Scripture. The Vulgate is largely from his pen.

A psychologist might say that Jerome, and many others like him, were driven by anxiety and guilt; that mystical visions were the symbolic reinstatement into consciousness of repressed material; that seeing impurity and carnality in others was the mechanism of reaction formation and that pious scholarship represented sublimation. Was Jerome's attitude toward women a subconscious mother fixation and might he have been a latent homosexual?

Monasticism was given order and direction by St. Benedict (about 480-543) who formalized a *rule of life* enabling like-minded people to live together in communities rather than separately as hermits. This was at the beginning of the Dark Ages, Rome had fallen and barbarians were pressing in on all sides. Presently the only places where reading and writing were practiced to any extent were the monastaries. As time went on they became extremely wealthy and great landowners. The rule of Benedict relaxed and now it seemed that Satan had taken over the monastic houses.

A group of people cannot say "I believe in poverty, chastity, and obedience" and then continue indefinitely on the road to wealth, fornication, and disobedience. Dissonance theory predicts that sooner or later there will be either a change in creed or a return, in practice, to the original ideals of the system. Characteristically, a reform movement gets under way when the actions of a group have departed to a considerable extent from the enshrined belief system of that group. The more firmly entrenched and zealously guarded the creed, the less likely it is to be changed, so under these circumstances reformers emerge who preach a return to the sterling virtues of the "good old days." Dissonance is reduced by making what I do consistent with what I say.

Early in the thirteenth century a wave of purification and reform was set in motion by a Spaniard, Dominic and by his friend and colleague Francis of Assisi, who started mendicate orders of friars who walked barefooted with neither purse nor script preaching the Gospel to the poor. The Crusades had whetted European appetites for spices, silks, and satins, luxuries enjoyed by the nobility, by the Establishment, and the Abbot of the local monastery was of the Establishment. Now the ANTI-SATAN response was made by the friars; religious vagabonds who worked in the slums.

However, before long, they too began to suffer the corruptions of an established order. Friars preempted the teaching positions in the newly emerging universities, they argued among themselves, infringed upon the duties of the local parish priest, and finally started peddling indulgences, a practice which they had previously severely condemned.

In the prologue to *The Canterbury Tales*, Chaucer gives us a picture of one of these wandering friars, the Pardoner, who is a seller of indulgences. He says:

> His walet lay biforn him in his lappe,
> Bret-ful of pardoun come from Rome al hoot.
> A voys he hadde as smal as hath a goot.
> No berd hadde he, he never sholde have,
> As smothe it was as it were late y-shave;
> I trow he were a gelding or a mare.
> But of his craft, fro Berwik into Ware,
> Ne was ther swich another pardoner,
> For in his male he hadde a pilew-beer,
> Which that, he seyde, was our lady veyl:
> He seyde, he had a gobet of the seyl
> That seynt Peter hadde, when that he wente
> Up-on the see, til Jesu Crist him hente.
> He hadde a croys of latoun, ful of stones,
> And in a glass he hadde pigges bones.
> But with thise relikes, when that he fond
> A povre person dwelling up-on lond,
> Up-on a day he gat him more money
> Than that the person gat in monthes tweye.[1]

Let's see what this rather unintelligible passage looks like when "translated" into modern English prose:

> He carried his bag, stuffed full of pardons hot from Rome, before him on his lap. His voice was small and goatlike. He had no beard, and never would have; his face was as smooth as if freshly shaven. I believe he was a eunuch. But in his business, there was not another such pardoner from Berwick to Ware. For in his bag he had a pillowcase which he said had served as the veil of Our Lady; he claimed to have a piece of the sail with which St. Peter went to sea until Jesus Christ caught him. He had a metal cross embedded with stones, and also he had pig's bones in a jar. And with these same relics, when he found a poor parson living out in the country, he made more money in one day than the parson made in two months.[2]

Clearly Chaucer sees the need for reform which is the need to reduce dissonance. He takes a dim view of the traffic in relics and indulgences. Note that he is writing one hundred and thirty years before Luther nailed his ninety-five theses on the church door at Wittenburg. Peddling indulgences was a scandal long before Luther got around to making his protest.

With the advent of the Reformation both monks and friars were in disrepute; as a matter of fact, the entire apparatus of the Church was degenerating into a morass of corruption. At this point we find the expected ANTI-SATAN response coming from two directions. From Rome emerged the vigorous Counter-reformation spearheaded by the *Society of Jesus,* the dedicated and militant Jesuit congregation. To them Satan had moved North of the Alps and was becoming the evil genius of the Protestant countries. The Protestants, on the other hand, were very sure that Satan was residing at Rome and that the Pope was ANTI-CHRIST.

The periodic need for reform and purification is a characteristic of Western culture and it is surprising how many such movements originated outside the Church. During the fourteenth century a group of laymen in the Low Countries established themselves as the "Brethren of the Common Life," devoting their energies to personal piety and education and paving the way for the general acceptance of Protestantism in the North. Hieronymus Bosch may have been associated with the group. During the seventeenth century we find the phenomenon of pietism with its effect on John and Charles Wesley and the Methodists. It also influenced the Baptists, Moravians, Mennonites, Dunkers, Quakers, Shakers, and innumerable others. The common element for all these groups was personal holiness combined with a repudiation of the "flesh" (i.e., card-playing, dancing, drinking, the theatre, sometimes even coffee and tea). Anything that was "worldly" was sinful. In varying degrees these groups experienced visions, trances, and ecstasies, they were given to prophesy and suffered the gift of tongues. They practiced divine healing. The general trend was to drop out and separate; the Puritans sailed away to the Massachusetts Bay Colony, the Amish and Mennonites went into the back country of Pennsylvania, the Mormons took the long, hard road to Utah. One must choose between the evil of Sodom and Gomorrah and the higher life of holiness which leads one far, far away, perhaps into the desert.

Holiness, however, tends to lose its vitality as a group grows in numbers and wealth and as the problems of administration take time away from the quest of the beatific vision. I may be persuaded that Walden Pond is the place to live and that my diet should be locust and wild honey, but what will I do with my children and grandchildren? The Shakers solved the problem by not having children; celibacy was the rule. The Mennonites, Amish, and other "plain people" of Pennsylvania have established a separate culture in which their children grow up. To them it is "normal," yet we read that the younger generation is breaking away. What will happen to the children of people who have withdrawn to live in "hippie" communes? Can we expect the same evangelical zeal from the children of people who have been converted to Jehovah's Witnesses? The first generation operated on a door to door basis, now they are building buildings and establishing an organization. When will they own enough property so that they will be thought of as a *wealthy* sect?

Today we think of Christian Scientists as being a well-heeled (no pun intended) and respectable people. The ubiquitous reading room is quiet, restrained, and expensive. Sunday mornings one finds a sprinkling of Cadillacs outside their churches with a little knot of chauffeurs gathered out back under the elms.

This indigenous American movement represents the ultimate ANTI-SATAN response. It is pure idealism; Satan simply does not exist; sickness, sin, sorrow, and death are "errors" in the mind of man and have no reality if they are not admitted, and sometimes the best way to abolish someone is not to fight him but to ignore him, to make him a not-person.

The origins of Christian Science may be traced to Portland, Maine, where there lived a certain Phineas Quimby (1802-1866) who developed a considerable reputation as a faith healer. One of his patients was Mrs. Mary Baker Eddy from Boston who appropriated and extended his thinking, becoming a teacher and healer in her own right. The thing caught on, chiefly because people were not required to move to the desert, give up their earthly possessions, wear unusual costumes, be purified through manual toil, or practice celibacy. And pragmatically it worked; a great deal of benefit can be derived from exercises in spiritual healing irrespective of the theological context.

The ANTI-SATAN response is usually made when the conditions of existence are too soft, when the culture is old, sick, and degenerate. There is need for rigor, fitness, and discipline. Then there is a great welling up of the subconscious of a sense of guilt and personal unworthiness which drives the pure in heart to excesses of self-denial in preparation for their combat against Satan. Usually one can not have *both* guns and butter, schools *and* battleships, luxury *and* rigor. But with Mrs. Eddy there was no such thing as guilt, sin, and Satan; how typically American—to be able to have your cake and eat it too.

REFERENCES

1. W. W. Skeat (ed.), *The Complete Works of Geoffery Chaucer* (Oxford: Oxford University Press, 1912), pp. 427-428.
2. Lumiansky (trans.), *The Canterbury Tales* (New York: Simon and Schuster, 1948), p. 12.

CHAPTER IV

The Dark Ages

Saint Luke begins his story of the Nativity by saying: "And it came to pass in those days, that there went out a decree from Caesar Augustus, that all the world should be taxed."[1] In this context "all the world" was more than a figure of speech; indeed, it seemed that the Empire included all of the world that mattered. It was a stable world with good roads, just laws, and flourishing business. During the reign of Caesar Augustus a surprisingly small police force was able to maintain order in the city of Rome; the law worked and people respected it.

Four hundred years later the government was unable to send out a decree which would be effective beyond the next town, and finally, in 404, the imperial capital of the West was moved from Rome to Ravenna, a small fortified city on the northern shore of the Adriatic. The barbarians had crossed the Alps and were devastating Northern Italy. Three times Alaric and his Visigoths besieged the Eternal City and finally captured it in 410.

It is doubtful whether Romans of the third and fourth centuries realized that they were living during the "decline and fall of the Roman Empire." The process was much too slow; some years things were better and other years they were worse, but, after all, that's life. It seems there is a great need to believe in the immortality of the culture in which one lives and a person who teaches any other doctrine is likely

33

to be regarded as a traitor. Indeed, there is much evidence supporting the hope that *our* way of life will go on forever because it is a fact that every now and then things take a turn for the better.

Consider the reign of Marcus Aurelius (121-180) who was a no-nonsense, law-and-order strong man. He was successful in pushing back the barbarians. He came very close to the ideal of Philosopher-King, of one who was both wise and just. He was a living example of what he taught; fortitude, temperance, social involvement, virtue—all of the good things which had been preached by the Stoic philosophers of old. Interestingly enough, he was ruthless in his persecution of the Christians; they did not fit into his idea of world order.

The Empire was given a new lease on life under Diocletian* who reigned from 284 to 305. He was a genius at administration, reorganizing the entire structure of government by breaking large, unwieldly units down into smaller, more efficient ones. He attempted to curb inflation by imposing strict price controls on every possible commodity including labor. He found that the old silver coinage had been debased by using a core of copper in much the same way that today our quarters look like a little sandwich with a copper filling. Diocletian read this as one of the signs of the times and caused new sterling silver coins to be minted. He was honest, sincere, conscientious, and respected, an implacable enemy of vice and corruption. As we have previously noted** toward the end of his reign he attempted to stamp out and abolish Christianity, feeling that it was a subversive and un-Roman activity.

We have spoken of the relations between Constantine and the church; his other major claim to fame was building the great city of Constantinople to be the New Rome, a uniquely Christian city, orthodox, bejeweled, radiant, and exuding the odor of sanctity. It was also a uniquely Greek city and destined to become the capital of the Byzantine em-

---

* See p. 21, Chapter II.
** See p. 22, Chapter II.

pire which, unlike Hitler's Third Reich, would actually last a thousand years.

An empire with two capital cities may hang together under strong leadership, particularly if there is not too much difference in language and culture. For example, Peter the Great built St. Petersburg and moved the capital there from Moscow; there was no trouble in holding the empire together. However, there were many differences between the Latin West and the Hellenized East. The inevitable happened in 364 when the empire split into two parts with Rome the capital of the West and Constantinople of the East.

Byzantine culture deserves our attention because it possessed a continuity which was lacking in the West. It acted as a sort of storehouse of value; a treasury of civilization which was fed back into the West during times when it seemed as though the only light shining in the darkness of the Dark Ages came from the East.

One of the focal points of interaction between East and West was the city of Ravenna, the city of refuge where emperor Honorius Flavus had fled to escape from Alaric the barbarian. He was buried there in the Mausoleum of his sister Galla Placidia which can still be seen today. (Plate No. 4)

Here one finds certain innovations. Mosaic decoration had been used for thousands of years, chiefly on floors and to brighten up building exteriors using bits of colored marble and glazed terra cotta. Now we see the use of small pieces of brilliantly colored glass which gives an illuminated, shimmering effect. In the new technique the mosaic is applied to walls, columns, supports, and ceilings to completely transform the interior into a place of mystery and magic. In contrast, the exterior is extremely simple with no effort at decoration at all. One steps from the outside world of mundane reality into a transcendent world of otherness. This art form was to develop further in Byzantine culture but fell into disuse in the hands of the barbarian invaders of the West. It is particularly suitable to illustrate the Greek Orthodox emphasis on the divine nature of Christ and to act as the setting for the sacred

35

drama of the Holy Eucharist, the *mysterium tremendum* which was so holy that the miracle must be performed behind a screen or curtain. On the other hand, many of the barbarians were Arians* and may not have responded to the same sort of setting; their heritage had been worshipping under the great sky, in forests and groves of sacred trees, in open air structures like Stonehenge.

Honorius died in 425 to be succeeded by his nephew Valentinian III who was six years old at the time. At first under the regency of his mother Galla Placidia, and later when he made his own mistakes, most of the Western Empire was dismembered. Africa fell to the Vandals, Attila the Hun devastated Northern Italy, large areas of Spain and Gaul were lost, and Sicily was invaded. Following Valentinian's twenty-five years of rule we find the last gasping death agony of the Western Empire, another period of twenty-five years during which nine people successively occupied the Imperial throne. Ironically, the last one was a seventeen-year-old boy named Romulus who lasted less than a year. It had been a long time since the first Romulus who, with his brother Remus, had founded Rome.

When we speak of the Dark Ages we are referring to the West and the date usually given for their beginning is 476 when the Gothic chieftain Odoacer sacked Rome and captured Ravenna, which he made the capital of Italy with himself as king. There was now only one Emperor, the one at Constantinople. This gave rise to an ambiguous situation. Odoacer was, in fact, king of the Gothic tribes living in Italy, but much of the old Roman administrative system continued to function. Zeno, the emperor of the East thought, with some justification, that he was the rightful heir to the Western empire now that the throne was vacant. He perceived Odoacer as one of his subjects. Things went along well enough for a while until Zeno concocted a scheme to reunite the old empire and sent the king of the Ostergoths to "liberate" Italy. We now have the spectacle of two Goths fighting pitched battles against each other in Northern Italy, the prize being the city

---

* See p. 20, Chapter II.

of Ravenna, the key city of a dead empire to which neither of them had any legitimate claim. After three years of fighting, including a protracted siege, the city fell to Zeno's Goth, an extremely able and unscrupulous man named Theodoric.

Unlike Odoacer, who had started life as a penniless recruit in the Roman army, Theodoric was the son of a chieftain, and, as such, had been sent at seven years of age to the court at Constantinople as a hostage where he lived until he was seventeen. One assumes that during those ten impressionable years he absorbed much of the culture of the host country. He was an educated barbarian, an Arian Christian, and quite ruthless when it suited his purpose. For example, his first act upon capturing Ravenna was to murder Odoacer with his own hand, despite the fact that the terms of surrender had specified a general amnesty.

By this time, Zeno had died and Theodoric did not feel obliged to fulfill his original mission but, rather, decided to remain on at Ravenna as king of Italy, a position which he held for thirty years. Here is another example of a strong man who brought order out of chaos. During Theodoric's reign Italy enjoyed peace and prosperity in a world otherwise torn by strife. Under him, Ravenna became a city worthy of a national capital. He built the church of St. Apollinaire Nuovo which still stands intact today. It is an interesting blend of East and West. Its form is that of a basilica derived from the Roman municipal hall, its glowing mosaics are Greek. (Plate No. 5)

However, one of the mosaics, *The Last Supper,* shows Christ reclining at a typical Roman banquet table. Notice how He stands out from the others. He is twice their size and the only one wearing a colored robe. The twelve apostles are crowded into an impossibly small space; there is no attempt at realism, this is a type of pictorial shorthand, of symbolism where the observer knew what was being represented and did not need a realistic or three-dimensional effect in order to get the message. (Plate No. 6)

Theodoric died in 526. The next year at Constantinople another remarkable barbarian ascended the imperial throne,

Justinian the Great. He was of Slavonic extraction but became more Greek than the Greeks. Where his predecessor Zeno had failed he succeeded and reconquered almost all of the Mediterranean world for the Empire. He and his ex-prostitute wife Theodora ruled from Spain to Asia Minor, from the Alps to North Africa. This was the golden age of Byzantine culture. Italy became a province or exarchate of the Empire; the exarchate of Ravenna. From the imperial workshops at Constantinople came artisans who built the church of St. Vitale. Unlike the basilica this is a domed octagonal structure deriving from the architecture of tombs and mausoleums, a style particularly associated with the East and brought to full flowering by Justinian in his great church of Hagia Sophia in Constantinople. If for no other reason it is worth a visit to Ravenna to see the two great mosaics of Justinian and Theodora in St. Vitale. (Plate No. 7, Plate No. 8)

The Art Historian H. W. Janson says of these:

> (In the new emerging ideal of human beauty we see . . .) extraordinarily tall, slim figures, with tiny feet, small almond-shaped faces dominated by the huge, staring eyes, and bodies that seem to be capable only of slow ceremonial gestures and the display of magnificently patterned costumes. Every hint of movement or change is carefully excluded—the dimensions of time and earthly space have given way to an eternal presence amid the golden translucency of Heaven, and the solemn, frontal images seem to present a celestial rather than a secular court. This union of political and spiritual authority accurately reflects the "divine kingship" of the Byzantine Emperor. We are, in fact, invited to see Justinian and Theodora as analogous to Christ and the Virgin: the hem of Theodora's mantle is conspicuously embroidered with the three Magi carrying their gifts to Mary and the newborn King, and Justinian is flanked by twelve companions—the imperial equivalent of the twelve apostles.[2]

This is a good example of the "Caesaro-Papism" previously mentioned in the discussion of church and state.*

---

* See p. 23, Chapter II.

The mosaics of Ravenna also illustrate iconography or the symbolic use of pictures where the chief concern is to transmit information rather than create art for art's sake. It is a type of visual shorthand where a crowd is indicated by a cluster of heads, where the more important persons are shown as being larger, where a saint is labeled by having a halo propped up behind his head, just as much of a label as if he had a tag attached to his body reading "I am a saint." This is the sort of pictogram which one finds during times when few people can *read* written labels, they can only read the symbolism of the picture. The stories of Adam and Eve, of Jonah and the Whale, of the three Wise Men, of the Crucifixion and Resurrection, were all part of the oral tradition; people knew the stories, all they required was to be reminded of them by a sign, by a picture which said—look—this is the appropriate story for this particular time and place. This is a reminder, this will act as a focus for your devotions.

While the mosaics of Ravenna and Constantinople were glowing with a dim religious light, the lights in Western Europe were going out. Justinian maintained his empire only by dint of continuous warfare which depleted the population and impoverished the land. The old Roman families now found themselves the persecuted minority. During the fourth and fifth centuries the pagan Saxons invaded England; perhaps the legends about King Arthur started at this time; he may have been a hero who resisted. The savage Lombards moved south over Germany and Austria and then overran Italy. The Vikings and Norsemen were a terror on the seas.

One finds a certain pattern here; wandering nomadic hordes of tough, virile people pressing in from the outside upon older cultures of decadent city dwellers. The original Hebrew tribes move in from the desert to conquer the land of Caanan, Monguls and Manchus sweep down into the older culture of central China, Macedonians move down into Greece, and so it goes. At times the most pressing need for the peoples of the older, established cultures is simply one of physical survival. In Europe during the Dark Ages the problem was how to combat the ravages of Norsemen, how to fight the Lombards, what to do about the Vandals who were so bad that they have given their name to a word in our vocabulary meaning useless destruction.

When the Lombards entered Italy in 568, Pope John III appointed the three pre-Lenten Sundays for supplication against the impending peril. Conditions were so bad that we find a revival of the SON OF MAN response. The following prayer was written at that time:

> O Lord God,
> Who seest that we put not our trust
> In anything that we do;
> Mercifully grant that by thy power
> We may be defended against all adversity.[3]

Not putting trust in anything which one might do but rather calling upon a Higher Power for salvation and deliverance is typical of times cursed by extreme misery, deprivation, and suffering. Christianity had emerged from Judaism during such times, then as the culture became rich and had trouble digesting its own fat, the ANTI-SATAN response was evident; now we are back again looking toward Heaven for help. During these times a verse was added to the Litany:

> From the fury of the Norsemen,
> Good Lord deliver us.

A more practical response to insecurity and fear was the development of the feudal system which eventually became a well-ordered hierarchal structure of interdependent activities. Everyone knew his place and what he was supposed to do. The local Count or Baron, Abbot or Bishop, lived in a fortress on the top of a hill and when the alarm sounded the serfs would drive their cattle into the castle courtyard and then take up arms against the invader. In exchange for this protection they farmed the land, hewed the wood, and drew the water. This may have been an "Escape from Freedom"[4] but more likely it was an escape from danger into a relatively secure social system.

The organization did not stop at the local level; lesser nobility owed allegiance and duties to greater nobility and they in turn were theoretically servants of the King. At the apex, again theoretically, was the Pope. The political system of action was consistent with the belief system in which the Pope was the chief vassal, or vicar, of God. During times when the feudal system was working fairly well dissonance was low; all things fitted together in a logical framework of reference.

So far we have had nothing but bad things to say about the barbarians, but our Western culture is a synthesis of contributions made by Goths, Franks, Celts, Saxons, Vandals, Lombards, and Norsemen on the one hand and remnants left over from the Ancient World on the other with Byzantine culture sometimes acting as a catalyst. What did the Barbarians contribute and when did they stop being barbarians?

The most obvious contribution was energy, drive, challenge, and new blood. One suspects that they had a considerable need for achievement. There is an interesting study to be done here. Aronson[5] postulates that this need can be measured by studying a person's doodles or scribbles and McClelland[6] has applied the technique to the study of ancient Greek pottery fragments under the assumption that designs used in decoration are analogous to doodles and will reflect the need for achievement in the culture which produces them. These studies have been very carefully conducted and present convincing evidence that there was a difference in decorative motif between the early, expanding period of Greek civilization and the later period of decline and that the difference in decoration is analogous to the difference in doodling between people who measure high and low on independent tests for the need for achievement. Briefly, some of the characteristics of doodles made by people with high achievement motivation are clear, discrete lines, and geometric configurations. This is characteristic of barbarian art. They decorated every possible surface of weapons, utensils, and other portable objects with geometric designs, many of them having clear, sharp angles, and discrete S-shaped curves.

Look at the pagan Norse carving of "A Dragon's Head" done in the early ninth century; part of the prow of a Viking ship. (Plate No. 9)

As certain pagan tribes were converted to Christianity they produced missionaries who set out with great zeal to convert other pagans. A focus for this activity was Ireland and from monastic centers in the Emerald Isle went forth missionary saints who undertook the conversion of Northern Europe. Look at the title page of the "Book of Kells" which was produced about the year 800. Notice the sharp, discrete angles and the geometric configurations, the great need for achievement. (Plate No. 10)

We may say that barbarians ceased from being barbarians when they became Christians and when some of them learned to read and write; when they developed a synthesis between their own culture and that of the Latin West. This was the wind blowing over Europe from the North. From the South and East came the vigorously expanding Moslem culture and in between, in their own little pocket, was the Byzantine Empire. Medieval Europe developed out of an interaction between these influences.

REFERENCES

1. *Holy Bible*, KJV. Luke, 2:1.
2. H. W. Janson, *History of Art* (New York: Prentice-Hall) and (Harry N. Abrams, Inc., 1962), pp. 170-171.
3. The Book of Common Prayer. Collect for Sexagesima, p. 120.
4. E. Fromm, *Escape from Freedom* (New York: Holt, Rinehart and Winston, 1941).
5. E. Aronson, "The Need for Achievement as Measured by Graphic Expression," *Motives in Fantasy, Action and Society*, D. C. McClelland (ed.) (Van Nostrand, 1958), pp. 249-269.
6. *Ibid.*, "The Use of Measures of Human Motivation in the Study of Society," McClelland, pp. 518-554.

CHAPTER V

The Gothic Paradox

"A paradox, A Paradox, / A most ingenious paradox!"
sings the chorus in *The Pirates of Penzance*. This foolish situation contrived by Sir W. S. Gilbert involves a twenty-one-
year-old Hero who was born on the twenty-ninth of February
in Leap Year. Therefore he has had only five birthdays.
Therefore if he wishes to calculate his age by birthdays he
is only a little boy of five! On the other hand, a small voice
within him tells him that he is *really* a young adult. Can he be
both at the same time?

This is amusing and no tension is generated; incongruence
is humorous as long as no one gets hurt. A mild amount of
inconsistency is stimulating and adds spice to life. A moustache
on the Mona Lisa is funny as long as it is not the symptom
of a serious disease.

But when the play is being acted on the stage of life,
when an entire population is in the cast, and when everyone
believes that the paradox is real, that there are actually two
states of reality, then there is likely to be dissonance.

We have seen the development of a theological-philosoph-
ical dualism between worldly and spiritual matters. This was
implicit in the theology of St. Paul in the first century, then
made explicit by St. Augustine early in the fourth century.
In his *City of God* he developed the idea of dual citizenship;
man is a citizen of both the heavenly Jerusalem, which is
above and is the mother of us all, and of the World, which
is a temporary state-of-affairs located here below. This thought
is central to developing Christian orthodoxy. Man was seen

43

as a sojourner here on earth orienting his life toward death when he could climb back up the spiritual umbilical cord which had never been completely severed. But he could not do this on his own, he needed help from the church, the saints, and the Blessed Virgin. Invisible hands would reach down to him. The focal point for this activity was the high altar at church, the point of interaction between the two worlds. It was the Church Militant, people in Holy Orders, who cared for the sick, registered births and deaths, made out wills, engaged in "progressive" agriculture, copied manuscripts, and acted as the only cement holding the remnants of civilization together. They were the only civil service and usually the only ones who could read and write the universal language which was Latin.

Another common element spread over the West was the presence of architectural and engineering works left from the ancient world. The ruins were not nearly as ruined then as they are today; aqueducts continued to carry water, the Roman roads were still the best ones available, and the marble facings of the baths and palaces of Rome were still in place. As a matter of fact, it was not until the Renaissance that energetic builders "mined" the city, stripping away the marble in order to use it for their own designs. These reminders of the glories of antiquity continued to haunt people and to perpetuate at least the idea of a strong universal state.

On Christmas day in the year 800 the idea was translated into action when the Pope crowned Charlemagne, the king of the Franks, Emperor of Rome. Now, once more, there were two Emperors, but it is interesting to note that the one in the East crowned himself and appointed the Patriarch (or Pope) while the reverse situation held in the West. There would be a long history of conflict between Emperor and Pope in the West.

The territory ruled over by Charlemagne was much smaller than that of Caesar Augustus who had sent out a decree that all the world should be taxed. The new Empire consisted of, roughly, what is now France, Germany, and Northern Italy.

Meanwhile in the East a new star had arisen in the person

44

of the prophet Mohammed whose direct, simple, monotheistic faith had been spread by zealous followers over a vast area stretching from Spain to India. There was no paradox here; no dualism; there was one God and Mohammed was his prophet; life on earth was to be lived to the hilt and after death the faithful looked forward to a paradise of hedonistic delights.

There were now three foci of culture; Rome, Constantinople, and Baghdad the Golden where a successor to the Prophet, Harun al-Rashid, ruled an empire bigger than the other two put together. Rome and Baghdad exchanged embassies; one of Harun's gifts to Charlemagne was an elephant which excited much curiosity in Rome.

The revived Roman empire under Charlemagne seemed like a step in the direction of law and order, but it fell apart after his death. However, the *idea* of an emperor persisted, and presently we find three generations of Germans named Otto occupying the imperial throne. The first one, whose wife was the daughter of a Saxon king of England back in the days before the Norman conquest, was crowned by the Pope in 962. His grandson, Otto III, died fighting in Northern Italy in 1002. The Ottonian period was a "little renaissance," a small burst of creative activity, a flickering gleam in the darkness. By now all of the barbarians had been converted to Christianity; they had stopped wandering about and had settled on the land. The feudal system was well established; God was in heaven, the Pope was in Rome, from time to time there was a Holy Roman Emperor and the world seemed safe and secure. Perhaps for some people life was dull; working on a farm for the lord of the manor was not as stimulating as being a sea rover. People missed going on adventures.

The urge to be up and doing gradually asserted itself, however, and by the end of the first millenium Europe was coming alive with an irritable, questing restlessness. William of Normandy invaded England in 1066. A contemporary record of this event is the Bayeux Tapestry. (Plate No. 11)

Here we see a lively and animated series of cartoon-like drawings which tell a story of conquest. Ships, buildings, and

45

people are all out of proportion, but that sort of realism is unimportant; this is simply a storytelling device using pictorial shorthand. And this is a story of the doings of real men in the real world of events. Unlike religious art it is not concerned with the life of the world to come. This is a story of human achievement.

Do we see evidence of the need for achievement in the sharp, clear, distinct figures? A detailed analysis of this would be of interest from the standpoint of Aronson and McClelland.* William's expedition was neither a long shot nor a sure thing; he entered a risk-taking situation with the probability of success about fifty-fifty; he maintained direct control of the operation; his motivation to succeed was greater than his motivation to avoid failure.

This "William the Conqueror" response is so very different from dropping out and retreating to the desert to wage war against Satan and it is almost the complete opposite from the SON OF MAN response. No doubt William had many masses said for the success of his venture, but this was more like taking out insurance; if anyone needed help from Heaven it was King Harold of England, and this was not forthcoming.

General dissatisfaction and the urge to go questing reached a climax in 1096 when, as a result of the preaching of Pope Urban II and Peter the Hermit, over 200,000 Europeans; clergy, nobility, knights, squires, yeomen, peasants, and vagabonds, set forth on the great venture to free the Holy Land from the rule of the Turks. The first Crusade had many and far-reaching consequences. The West was introduced to newer and more complete translations of Aristotle, to a new number system, to advances in medical practice, and to a more sophisticated way of life. Merchants began to come into their own with the increased demand for silks, satins, spices, and other luxury items.

Today, the word *crusade* evokes various images; one thinks of Billy Graham in Madison Square Garden or a drive for moral rearmament conducted by a group of wholesome

---

* See p. 41, Chapter IV.

young people. The original Crusade was more like an adventure, a colossal boy scout hike. Everyone knew that it was God's will, it was a good thing which was sure to produce spiritual benefits, but at the same time, it was daring and exciting, it got people out of the rut of everyday humdrum existence. Crusaders returned with wild tales of far-off places. During subsequent expeditions to the Holy Land the spiritual element tended to fade into the background. One of the attractions was the opportunity to plunder Constantinople on the way, and many crusaders never got farther.

We may regard this sort of crusading as an early symptom of the drive toward discovery, exploration, conquest and empire which was to manifest itself so powerfully later on.

Meanwhile, Europe was starting to demand things which only commerce and trade could supply. Of particular interest was the great demand for relics which acted as a focus for devotion and good luck charms. It has been estimated that if all the splinters of wood purporting to be parts of the "True Cross" had been piled together they would have filled a large cathedral. Traveling entrepreneurs did a brisk business in all sorts of material: nails from the Cross, bits of the spear which had pierced the side of the Saviour, swatches of cloth from His seamless robe, bits of bone, flasks of tears, hanks of hair from the beard of some saint, and so on ad nauseum. Not everyone was taken in, there were people like Chaucer who took a dim view of this sort of activity.* Recall what a miserable picture he paints of the *Pardoner,* besides selling indulgences the wretched creature also had for sale pigs' bones which he palmed off as relics.

The cult of relics served the same purpose during the age of faith that the cult of a national flag served later during the age of nationalism and that the embalmed body of Lenin serves today. Surely, here is the best preserved and most impressively displayed relic of all time and the hundreds of thousands of pilgrims who visit this shrine each year emerge with the same expressions of pious devotion that one might

---

* See pp. 29-30, Chapter III.

see on the faces of Christian pilgrims emerging from some holy shrine.

The cult of relics is a response closely related to the cult of martyrs. Usually the relic is part of the body of a martyr or something intimately associated with his life. It is recorded that at the execution of Charles I there was a scramble to get under the scaffold and dip handkerchiefs in the blood. Now this *may* have been nothing more than souvenir hunting, but then, what is the difference between a souvenir and a relic? They both help one to remember, and, if later on, the thing remembered takes on spiritual significance, the souvenir becomes a relic, a focus for devotion, a secondary reinforcement for faith, and as we enter the Middle Ages we enter what is known as the *age of faith.*

It was not a stagnant age. At the same time that the Crusades were in progress some of the great European universities were being founded; Oxford in 1100 and Paris in 1169. Closely associated with the growing intellectual life of Paris was the great medieval scholar Abelard who may be considered as typical of the best of the so-called "twelfth century renaissance." Born in Brittany in 1076, just ten years after William the Conqueror sailed to England, he moved to Paris as a young man where he spent most of his life helping to create the climate out of which the university was to emerge 27 years after his death in 1142. His famous romance with one of his students, Heloise, resulted in her pregnancy and, as a consequence, her guardian had the professor castrated. Subsequently he entered a monastic order and she became a nun. Times have changed.

Despite his personal tragedy Abelard was anything but castrated in his mental processes; he was a champion of the power of human reasoning and argued persuasively for a logical foundation for Christian doctrine. He was concerned about the source of responsibility in human actions, it was human *intention* which made behavior good or bad. Here we find the small beginnings of a motivational psychology and a turning away from mysticism.

As a theologian Abelard skirted the edge of heresy and

was in continual disputation with his more orthodox brethren in the Church. His most powerful opponent was Bernard of Clairvaux. Saint Bernard (Abelard never made it) was a very eloquent proponent of mystical faith which transcends reason; of the Holy Paradox.

We can pinpoint the origin of Gothic architecture, under the direct influence of St. Bernard, with the dedication of the reconstructed Abbey Church of St. Dennis outside Paris in 1144, two years after the death of Abelard. Some of the tensions which developed in the "Gothic System" derive from the divergent views of Abelard on the one hand and St. Bernard on the other. (Plate No. 12)

In the "typical" Gothic cathedral most of the walls have been replaced by mysteriously glowing stained glass and the ceiling has become an upthrusting forest of arms and branches reaching out toward the life of the world to come.

Out of the trunk-like supporting columns peer the faces of Saints, their elongated bodies half emerging from the stone out of which they are carved. Over the doorways are vivid scenes of the Last Judgment complete with monsters and demons. Monsters and demons also perch on the towers and water spouts have become gargoyles. The entire structure seems poised for a take-off into space, lifted up by the giant fingers of its flying buttresses even as the fingers of the priest elevate the Host at mass.

The principal centers of learning were moving from the confines of the monastery to the more public Cathedral Schools; hence the term Schoolmen and the derived word Scholasticism. The early phase of this activity is well represented by Abelard; more mature and developed Scholasticism is exemplified by Albertus Magnus (1193-1280) and Thomas Aquinas (1225-1274). Both men were members of the Dominican order but they were not cloistered behind monastery walls, they moved about in the world of everyday events. Both men were recognized as great scholars during their lifetime.

Albertus Magnus fulfilled the difficult dual role of being both scientist and theologian, while Thomas Aquinas was more

49

the philosopher-theologian. Thomas, the younger man, "went to school" under Albertus at Cologne for three years where he became the master's chief disciple. Together they traveled to Paris where they became outstanding scholars at the University. They represent the high tide of Scholasticism when heroic efforts were made to reconcile the dichotomy between the natural world of empirical observation and the supernatural world of revealed religion.

Albertus translated and commented on many of the works of Aristotle, adding new information from his own observations of nature. He offered natural explanations for many phenomena including the existence of fossils, the origin of volcanoes, the source of rivers, erosion of the land, the flow of sap in trees, and the embryonic nature of seeds. Bear in mind that this was all done at a time when naturalistic observation bordered on heresy.

Of interest to psychologists today, Albertus contributed the important thought that the chief difference between man and animal was that the former had a rational soul while the latter only a sensitive soul, in other words, both man and animal had the power to make responses to stimulation in their environment, but only man was possessed of the ability to use the higher mental processes of abstraction, concept formation, reasoning, willing, and making plans for the future.

Albertus' younger contemporary, Thomas Aquinas, was a saint and mystic on the one hand and a rational philosopher on the other. He took over from Aristotle the notion of a self-contained system of universal knowledge; all things fit together in a logical framework of reference. He wrote careful and detailed commentaries on Aristotle's works on the soul, memory, ethics, the senses, physics, and metaphysics. This natural and rational system, so logical and complete, did not, however, include a category in which orthodox Christian theology could comfortably fit, and this was the task to which St. Thomas set himself in his stupendous master-work, *Summa Theologica,* upon which he labored between 1266 and 1273, the year before his death.

In the Thomastic synthesis we find the rational human

intellect coming out from God the creator. Divine truth is absolute, but the individual soul is free to *will* assent or rejection. He calls this choice a *movement* of the will. (One thinks of Otto Rank's *Will Therapy* and Kurt Lewin's *Locomotion in a Life Space*.) Such movement, if it be toward divine truth, is assisted by a force emanating from God which he calls *Grace*. Grace is special help and fortitude which is imparted as the result of living within the full sacramental system of the Church. Sin is the "wrong" choice or movement away from God. Grace, however, like the Peace of God, remained something that passeth understanding.

St. Thomas maintained that the study of natural science is in no way a wrong choice because the laws of nature are God's laws. Free speculation is not inconsistent with faith because faith sharpens and gives direction to reason. By reason alone man can arrive at the logical necessity of a First Cause, of an Unmoved Mover, and this is God. Given this, the entire structure of Catholic theology may be logically deduced. It is reasonably necessary that the Godhead exist in three persons and that the second person of this Trinity be the Saving Victim of the New Testament.

But the rational Thomas was still St. Thomas the mystic. In 1263 he wrote the beautiful hymn, *Martyr Dei*:

> O saving Victim, opening wide
> The gate of heaven to man below,
> Our foes press on from every side,
> Thine aid supply, thy strength bestow.
>
> All praise and thanks to thee ascent,
> Forever more, blest One in Three;
> O grant us life that shall not end,
> *In our true native land with thee*. (italics added)[1]

This last line well illustrates the Gothic paradox. Here below our foes, Satan and his minions, press on from every side but our real citizenship is not here, it is in the true native land which is the City of God. If we make it, it will be by the grace of God—"Thine aid supply, thy strength bestow."

Many Gothic paintings are vivid illustrations of this. There was no such thing as "art for art's sake" any more than there had been in the mosaics of Ravena or the Bayeux Tapestry, and many of the earlier paintings were anonymous. We know them today simply by region and approximate date such as "Florentine School, XIII Cent." Actually "school" here might better be rendered "workshop" because these painters were craftsmen turning out orders commissioned for the decoration of churches. A good example is the icon-like *Virgin with Child* by a thirteenth century Florentine. (Plate No. 13)

It is highly stylized and full of distortions. Look at the unnatural angle of the mother's head and her long, worm-like fingers, particularly the index finger of her left hand. The baby's gesture of benediction and his very small head make him look like a miniature adult. The shape of Mary's face, her conventionally drawn features, and rather blank expression are stereotypes to be found in thousands of other Gothic paintings. This is the symbolic representation of an idea; a pictograph in which there is no effort to show real people engaging in some recognizably normal activity. Byzantine influence is strong.

The next painting was done about a generation later by Duccio Di Boninsegna (1255-1318). We see Mary dressed in the same blue garment, identical even to the little medallions on the right shoulder and hood. Her neck is at the same angle and she has the same features which are echoed in the faces of the six small angels supporting her throne. The *size* of the baby indicates that he is not more than eighteen months old while his *proportions* are those of a child of eight. One wonders whether the artist was incapable of drawing a realistic baby or whether he was not supposed to because convention dictated otherwise. Perhaps the Son of Man and the Saving Victim should not be represented as a weak and helpless creature. (Plate No. 14) This is a very large painting intended to go behind an altar. The golden glow of the background is typical. This is entirely the heavenly condition of St. Thomas' "true native land"; there is no air to breathe, no earth to walk on, no environment in which a living person could reasonably exist.

The painting by Cimabue (1240-1302) was done about 1280. It is identical to the previous one in almost every respect except that Cimabue has included four "prophets," little human figures at the very bottom of the picture.

The two center ones look quite normal but those at either end seem to need the services of a chiropractor; their necks are impossibly twisted. (Plate No. 15)

Finally, we come to Giotto (1267?-1337), one of the last great Gothic painters and architects, one who prefigured the Renaissance in many of his works. This painting is of the same stereotyped subject matter, done for people who told him exactly what they wanted, but the artist has added something of his own. (Plate No. 16) The scene is no longer completely flat; instead of being pasted on her throne like a cutout, Mary seems to be actually sitting on it, she is occupying real space and the throne is drawn with some notion of linear perspective. The saints and angels in the background are placed one behind the other as if they might be standing on real ground rather than suspended in a vacuum.

Giotto was a friend and contemporary of Dante and both thought of themselves as "moderns." During his journey through Purgatory, Dante has one of his characters say that:

> Once, Cimabue thought to hold the field
> In painting; Giotto's all the rage today;
> The other's fame lies in the dust concealed.[2]

Dante Alighieri (1265-1321) and his friend Giotto were two great Gothic figures living near the end of their epoch. Dante, the poet, in his *Divine Comedy,* takes us on a tour of the after-life from the lowest pit of Hell up into the "true native land" of Paradise. In the fifth heaven of eternal sunlight Dante encounters a group of holy wise men, those who have been illuminated. Their spokesman is none other than St. Thomas (Thomas of Aquino) and standing at his right hand is Albertus Magnus (Albert of Cologne). Thomas introduces himself to Dante:

> Lamb of the holy flock was I, obeying
> Dominic on that road he led us by,
> Where is good fattening is there be no straying.

> Brother to me and master, one stands nigh
> On my right hand here; Albert of Cologne
> Was he, and Thomas of Aquino, I.[3]

Dante was a statesman-politician as well as a poet, one of the newer breed of intellectuals who were not members of a monastic order. He was not above assigning political enemies to particularly horrible tortures in the nether depths of the *Inferno;* like the Mikado, he had an ingenious way of "making the punishment fit the crime."

However, what Dante the psychologist is doing is to present his readers with an allegory; the journey from Inferno through Purgatory to Paradise is really a pilgrimage in this life on earth from misery through various purgations and vicissitudes to a state of enlightenment, peace and felicity; to self-actualization. It can be done here and now by real people living in the real world, by people having free-will and the gift of reason, by people whose actions determine what they are to become. Dante sums up the medieval point of view and looks forward to the dawn of a new age when the focus will be on Man the Doer.

REFERENCES

1. Op. cit. *The Hymnal of the Protestant Episcopal Church.* Hymn 209, St. Thomas Aquinas, 1236. Tr. Edward Caswall, 1849.
2. Dante, *Purgatory*, Canto XI, v. 94, Penguin Books, 1955. p. 152. Tr. Dorothy L. Sayers.
3. Dante, *Paradise*, Canto X, v. 94 & 95, Penguin Books, 1962. pp. 137-138. Tr. Dorothy L. Sayers and Barbara Reynolds.

Plate Number 17:   "The Deposition" Giotto, Arena Chapel, Padua.

Plate Number 18: "Madonna and Child with St. Anne", Masaccio, Uffizi.

Plate Number 19: "Madonna and Child with Angels", Filippo Lippi, Uffizi.

Plate Number 20: "Allegory of Spring", Botticelli, Uffizi.

Plate Number 21: "Madonna of the Magnificat", Botticelli, Uffizi.

Plate Number 22: "Birth of Venus", Botticelli, Uffizi.

Plate Number 23: "Calumny of Apollo", Botticelli, Uffizi.

Plate Number 24: "Deposition", Botticelli, Pinacotheque, Munich.

Plate Number 25:   "Pope Leo X and his Nephews", Raphael, Pitti
Palace, Florence.

Plate Number 26: "Madonna of the Harpies", Andrea del Sarto, Uffizi.

Plate Number 27: "Madonna of the Long Neck", Parmigianino, Uffizi.

Plate Number 28: "Presentation of the Virgin", Tintoretto, Santa Maria dell' Orto, Venice.

Plate Number 29: "Last Judgment", Michelangelo, Vatican, Sistine Chapel.

Plate Number 30:   Detail from "Last Judgment", *Christ as Righteous Judge*, Vatican, Sistine Chapel.

Plate Number 31: "Baptism of Christ", El Greco, Madrid, Prado, (the lower part of the painting).

Plate Number 32: "Burial of Count Orgaz", El Greco, St. Tome, Toledo.

Plate Number 33: "Landscape with Burial of Phocion", Poussin, The Louvre.

Plate Number 34: "The Garden of Love", Rubens, Prado.

Plate Number 35: Photograph, *Colonnade in front of St. Peter's*, Bernini, Vatican.

Plate Number 36: "A Pilgrimage to Cytheria", Watteau, The Louvre.

CHAPTER VI

Humanism

When a belief system is no longer relevant to the facts of existence, when its custodians have become weak and when reform seems like an impossible task, one finds changes in belief in the direction of dissonance reduction.

We would argue that one of the "causes" of the Renaissance was the inadequacy of the medieval belief system to explain or contain the expanding world of reality. In the last chapter it was pointed out that intellectually and religiously the Gothic world was dualistic, that man lived in a compromise condition of double citizenship. This worked for a while until people began to discover that the earth was larger and more complex than had been previously supposed. Marco Polo brought home tales of wonder, Portuguese navigators discovered the dim Azores and began pushing down the West coast of Africa, the smell of gun-powder was in the air, and the divinely sanctioned feudal system was showing signs of strain. National governments were becoming stronger, an artisan and mercantile middle class was emerging, and in many city states BUSINESS was the order of the day.

The paradoxically dualistic medieval world had generated a need for unity, for a fixed point of view and coherence; now we find the painter and architect achieving order through mathematical perspective. This was consistent with the good order of sonnet form in poetry, with the polished and logical oration, with careful accounts and sound business practices, and politically with what Jacob Burckhardt calls "The State as a Work of Art."[1] This was consistent with humanism which proclaimed confidence in mankind and tended to be anticlerical, skeptical, and sophisticated.

Humanism did not reach down into the masses but was rather a climate of thinking among intellectuals. Petrarch (1304-1374) is a good example. A younger contemporary of Dante and Giotto, he was a man who also removed himself from the medieval point of view. He sought inspiration from the classics of antiquity, from the ghost of ancient Rome which had died but persisted in living on. He wrote extensively in Latin and Italian, the latter language being the vehicle for his famous *Sonnets to Laura*. The romantic ideal supports a certain humanizing influence; Abelard and Heloise, Dante and Beatrice, and now Petrarch and Laura; love is such a very human thing.

Petrarch led a restless, questing existence, never living for more than a few years in one place, moving about on diplomatic missions, visits to his friend Boccaccio, poetry readings at Paris or Rome, retreats to the country and flights from the plague, until he was found dead one morning, seated in his library, with his head resting on his favorite copy of Virgil.

Petrarch's humanism consisted in his sensitive portrayal of the needs and ambitions, of the joys and sorrows, of man; of man living here on earth having experiences in the world of everyday reality; of man existing in an intelligible framework of reference.

Considerably more human than the Petrarch-Laura type of love is the tender passion according to Boccaccio (1313-1375) which is nothing more or less than down to earth sex. For example, one of the hundreds of little descriptions from the *Decameron* reads:

> They passed a delicious night, and the nightingale sang ever so many times. Heated at last by the weather and their sport, they fell asleep without any covering over them, Caterina having her right arm under her lover's neck, and holding in her left hand what modesty forbids me to name before ladies.[2]

This is a far cry from the mystical ecstasies of someone

like St. Francis of Assisi; the only stigmata that the disciples of Boccaccio were likely to acquire were the stigmata of syphilis.

Humanism began the process of secularizing scholarship, once the sole province of the clerical order. It coincided with a vigorously renewed interest in the ancient world of Greece and Rome. It focused upon man as a citizen of the real existential world rather than as a citizen of the heavenly world above. The new art was something to be enjoyed as well as serving as an aide to devotion. There was a revival of hedonism; the notion that pleasure and aesthetic satisfaction is the natural goal of mortal man.

As the 14th century drew to a close people looked back on an era during which hundreds of thousands of men, women and children, saints and sinners alike, had died of the Great Plague, the Black Death which neither church nor state had the slightest power to mitigate. Some said that the Jews had poisoned the wells, others said that it was a visitation of divine wrath, and still others that it was due to bad air, but burning the ghettoes, propitiatory acts of devotion, and spraying the air with infusions of herbs all seemed equally ineffective. This must have generated a very high level of anxiety, indeed, anxiety sometimes on the border of hysteria and panic. The late medieval preoccupation with death began at this time, the focus was shifting from the after-life to the fact of human mortality. One response was to "eat, drink and be merry, for tomorrow ye die."

Another factor influencing the lives of Europeans in the wake of the plague was the Great Schism; the visible decline of the great spiritual power of the papacy. Between 1378 and 1429 Europe was treated to the scandalous spectacle of rival popes; at first there were two, then toward the end, actually three contenders for the throne of St. Peter. Today we commemorate this every time we drink a bottle of that excellent wine known as *Chateau neuf du pape,* or "New home of the Pope." The wine is produced in the country about Avignon where one of the papal courts was established.

The late Gothic world existed in high dissonance. There

were inconsistencies between the traditional belief system and events which were actually taking place. One expects to find dissonance reducing responses in the form of changed belief, changed action, or both as the culture jockeys and maneuvers toward a new Gestalt in which all of the arts of the mind and hand are in mutual support of each other.

In this context humanism is presented as a change in belief but not as a belief *system*. Humanism is an attitude or orientation of the mind which was strictly occidental; a non-oriental orientation. Eastern cultures have generally placed little value on notions of human rights while for us in the West there are ideas and ideals which make us vaguely uncomfortable when we see serfs, slaves, and beggars. Poverty in a world of plenty is inconsistent.

Some of these typically Western trends in thinking are reflected in the words *humane* and *humanitarian,* in such instruments as the *Magna Charta* and the *Bill of Rights,* in such organizations as the *League of Nations* and the *United Nations,* in *Social Security* and the idea of a *Welfare State,* in enterprises like *Public Health* and *Medicare,* art galleries, libraries, museums, lectures, and concerts, all of which are supported by public funds, in the idea that the primary role of government is to render service to people. To what extent do expensive moon voyages contribute to this ideal?

Many names come to mind in this connection. One thinks of Jean Jacques Rousseau, Thomas Jefferson, Jeremy Bentham, John Stuart Mill—the list could go on and on including all of the "old-fashioned liberals," many of the Romantic poets, and the "transcendentalists" who lived when Boston was the "Athens of America." All of this is far removed from the life and times of Petrarch and Boccaccio, and there are many counter-examples, Hitler and Stalin were not outstanding as humanists or humanitarians, yet a concern for humanity is a feature of Western culture and it is doubtful whether we would have as much as we do today if it had not been for late Gothic and Renaissance humanism.

The heritage of humanism includes such men as Thomas Gray (1716-1771) who sang of "The short and simple annals of the poor" and observed that "The paths of glory lead but to the grave." He did not like people who would . . . "wade through slaughter to a throne, and shut the gates of mercy on mankind."[3] It includes Jeremy Bentham (1748-1832) who believed that a social system ought to provide "the greatest good for the greatest number of people" and it also includes Bentham's friend and pupil John Stuart Mill (1806-1873) who, in his *Essay on Liberty* wrote:

> The object of this Essay is to assert one very simple principle, as entitled to govern absolutely the dealings of society with the individual in the way of compulsion and control. . . . That principle is that the sole end for which mankind are warranted, individually and collectively, in interfering with the liberty of action of any of their number, is self-protection. That the only purpose for which power can be rightfully exercised over any member of a civilized community, against his will, is to prevent harm to others. His own good, either physical or moral, is not sufficient warrant. He cannot rightfully be compelled to do or forbear because it will make him happier, because, in the opinion of others, to do so would be wise, or even right.[4]

Note that according to this rather old-fashioned point of view it would be proper to force a person to stop polluting the water supply because polluted water hurts other people, but we would not be permitted to force black children to travel great distances in order to attend a white school because it would be better for them and make them happier. Indeed this does seem to be an old-fashioned view-point, it is also contrary to the whole idea of compulsory public education.

Coming down to the present day, in direct line from Bentham and Mill, is the Fabian Society of England. Early Fabians included George Bernard Shaw, Beatrice and Stanley Webb. They were non-violent socialists whose major concern was Man and his role in the modern world. The English Labor Party is their step-child. Today they are actually sponsoring some psychological research: how far does man aspire to equality and a classless society?

We have barely scratched the subject; more will be said in chapter XI on "Neo Humanism." The only point to be made here is that humanism started a trend in Western thinking which has developed in many directions with many ramifications. Originally humanism was concerned with studying the classics, the values and achievements of great men from the golden ages of the past. Today the *humanities* consist in the study of art, music, literature, and the great achievements of the past. Today if a university wishes to honor a philanthropist he may be awarded the degree of D.H.L. or L.H.D., Doctor of Humane Letters or Doctor of Humanities. Today we speak of the humane treatment of prisoners and the insane, we have humane societies, animal rescue leagues, and societies for the prevention of cruelty to children and so on. This concern for life in general and human life in particular is unique to Western Culture. It is true that certain Hindu sects refuse to take life, even to kill insects, but their motive is a mystical-religious one involving a belief in reincarnation. In the West it is a reverence for life *per se* and is not predicated upon what might happen after death.

Here we see a major change in belief from the early Christian and medieval point of view. It did not come about all at once, it has many manifestations and aspects of it are still evolving today. When humanism is "working," that is, when humans behave as if faith in them were justified, dissonance is reduced to a comfortable level. But one wonders for how long man is able to act consistently with belief in himself as capable of acting. Reading history makes one rather cynical about this.

REFERENCES

1. Burckhardt, J., *The Civilization of the Renaissance in Italy*. Vol. I, Part I, "The State as a Work of Art." Harper Torchbooks, 1958.
2. Boccaccio, *The Decameron*, Novel LV of Fifth Day.
3. Gray, T., *Elegy Written in a Country Churchyard. The Standard Book of British and American Verse*. Garden City. 1932. pp. 189-193.
4. Mill, J. S., *Essay on Liberty*. Henry Holt, 1874, p. 23.

CHAPTER VII

The Need for Rebirth

As it became increasingly clear that the Gothic system was inadequate to offer explanations which would satisfy the "modern" intellectual, the satisfaction of curiosity became a powerful motive. People sought naturalistic explanations for phenomena. To climb a mountain simply because it was there or in order to enjoy the view from the top seems natural enough for us today, but at the outset of the Renaissance it was something which had not been done for over a thousand years. Now men started doing things simply for the sake of doing them.

The conviction grew that mankind had been going through a "middle age" and that now the dawn of a new age was at hand when civilization would awaken from its long sleep and take up where the ancient world had left off. The new age would be even better than the old one. Consciously and with self-awareness the need to be reborn was recognized.

Perhaps this is one of the key factors in the reawakening of Europe. We have said that people living during the Dark Ages were not aware that they were living in a dark age and that the ancient world ground slowly to a halt. It took a long time dying. By contrast we get the impression that the Renaissance came with somewhat of a bang and people were aware that they were awake and recognized their own needs for achievement.

It is one thing to understand the dynamics of motivation but it is another thing to bring together the circumstances which make the satisfaction of the need possible. Why do we find the first fruits of the Renaissance in north-central Italy and why was the city-state of Florence the focus for this activity?

It would give us much satisfaction if we could point out that it was because the citizens were living in a free and glorious democracy, self-actualizing themselves without inhibition or restraint. Such was not the case. It is true that cities such as Florence, Genoa, and Venice *had been* republics of one sort or another toward the end of the Middle Ages, but when creative activity really got started they had become oligarchies. The great banking and merchant families of Florence, the Strozzi, Pitti, Rucellai, and Medici held the government of the city securely in their hands. Early in the fifteenth century Cosimo de'Medici (1389-1464) emerged as the most powerful and gifted of these men and, after various skillful political maneuvers, became an absolute ruler known to posterity as "the Father of his Country." Cosimo had the wit to govern behind a facade of republican forms and never accepted the titles or symbols of monarchy. The dynasty continued under his son Piero who died after five years of rule to be succeeded in turn by his son, one of the great Renaissance figures, Lorenzo, known as "il Magnifico." He would accept no other title and continued to operate, as his grandfather Cosimo had done, using the outward forms of republican government.

The great Renaissance historian, Guicciardini (1483-1540) describes the life and times of Lorenzo in the first chapter of his *History of Florence*. Lorenzo did not die until 1492 when Guicciardini was nine years old, so that he was almost an eye-witness to the conditions described above. Note that 1492 was a key date in Western civilization; not only did Columbus discover the New World, but the Moors were expelled from Spain; Erasmus, the last great humanist, was ordained to the priesthood, and Lorenzo the Magnificent died, marking the end of an era in which, according to Guicciardini:

The city enjoyed perfect peace, the citizens were united and in harmony, and the government so powerful that no one dared oppose it. The people every day delighted in shows, revelries and other novelties; they were well fed, as the city was plentifully supplied with victuals, and all its activities flourished. Men of intellect and ability were contented, for all letters, all arts, all talents were welcome and recognized. . . . Principally for the study of letters he (Lorenzo) set up a university in Pisa, and when people argued that for many reasons there could never be as many students there as there had been at Pavia and Padua, he said it was enough for him if the teachers were the best in Italy. So in his lifetime all the best and most famous men in Italy taught there and were very highly paid, for no expense or trouble was spared to get hold of them. . . . He also equally favored poetry in the vernacular, music, architecture, painting, sculpture, and all the arts of the mind and hand, so that the city abounded in all such ornaments of life.[1]

Here, then, were the conditions under which the achievements of a Golden Age became possible. First, there was order and security provided by an efficient government, (the state as a work of art) and second, there were patrons, *rich* men, perceptive enough to collect geniuses. The creative person was protected, supported, and encouraged. When Lorenzo the Magnificent died in 1492 at the early age of forty-three, the eighteen-year-old Michelangelo was a member of his household.

It is of interest to note that John Stuart Mill's notion of *liberty* is not necessarily the condition under which creative genius makes its best response. Consider the last fifty years under the Czars. There have never been such composers as Tchaikovsky, Mussorgsky, Rimski-Korsakov, and Borodin; chemists like Borodin (the same man) and Mendelyeev; writers like Tolstoi, Dostoievski, and Turgenev; playwrights like Chekhov; physiologists like Pavlov. One might compile an impressive list of great men. The only thing that Imperial Russia and Medici Florence had in common was the availability of discriminating patrons; the government of Russia was ineffective and weak; that of Florence was efficient and strong. However, a strong government without patrons, like Hitler's, failed to produce any creative art. We will have to further examine the role of the patron.

Meanwhile back in Italy, let us look at some of the changes which took place in painting as the country began to experience the *need for rebirth*. Look once more at the *Madonna Enthroned* by Giotto (Plate No. 16) which was used to illustrate late Gothic art. We are looking exclusively at doings in heaven. Mary is disproportionately large to show that she is more important than the other figures who group themselves about her throne in a balanced and symmetrical design. The gold dinner-plate haloes of the *dramatis personae,* which seem to be suspended behind their heads, echo the flat gold background. The Madonna's expression is enigmatic and without emotion, almost like an ambiguous picture in a projective test. If the viewer feels guilt he may perceive her as gently chiding, if he needs to be comforted, the Holy Mother radiates comfort, if he is anxious, her face imparts serenity and confidence. She is abstract, ambiguous, and universal. This is the *mysterium tremendum* of eternal womanhood; compassion and understanding which transcend reason.

This is the Giotto who sums up the medieval point of view, the Giotto who looks forward to a new age as may be seen in his frescoes illuminating the walls of the Arena Chapel in Padua. (Plate No. 17) Here we see convincingly real people involved in an activity which is charged with emotion. These wall paintings were available to anyone who wished to study them and for art students they served the same purpose that museums do today.

Masaccio (1401-1428) must have studied them. He lived for only twenty-seven years yet he exercised a profound influence upon his and succeeding generations of painters. His *Madonna and Child with Saint Anne* is separated by about one hundred years from Giotto's *Madonna* and at first glance it does not seem that much progress has been made; we still have an other-worldly golden glow for the background and harvest-moon haloes behind every head. (Plate No. 18) The little angels are the same stereotyped creatures to be seen in thousands of Gothic paintings and the "action" is definitely not of this world. But try blocking out the angels and haloes and concentrate on the family group of grandmother, mother, and child; they are good solid figures occupying three-dimensional space, they are all lit from the same source of illumination which seems to shine over the viewer's left shoulder and the robes of the two women drape convincingly over what we know must be real flesh and bones. Grandmother is being protective, mother seems depressed and resigned to her fate, and baby looks more like a real baby than in previous paintings. It took a hundred years to go from Giotto to Masaccio, but now things seem to burst out all over as if some sort of critical mass had been reached.

Five years younger than Masaccio, there lived in Florence an orphaned boy named Filippo Lippi (1406-1469) who was "placed" with the Carmelites to become a monk. No doubt his taking religious orders was more for the convenience of his relatives than for any convictions on his part. In any event, brother Philip was more than a brother to a certain nun, sister Lucrezia, who bore him a son when he was fifty years old. The fruit of her womb was little Philip or Filippino Lippi, who, like his father, became a famous artist. Fra Filippo Lippi started his artistic training as a pupil of Masaccio, and in the course of time became a master in his own right and accepted students; one was his son Filippino and another was Sandro Botticelli, so if we start with Masaccio and end with Botticelli we will have a small sample of Florentine painters of the fifteenth century, during that period of time when the city enjoyed the peace and security of Medici rule.

Fra Filippo Lippi did his *Virgin and Child* about 1464, the year in which Cosimo de'Medici was succeeded by his son Piero. (Plate No. 19)

We see Mary sitting in a large open window which provides a view of rocky cliffs, fields, and lakes. The heavy gold haloes of Masaccio have become very thin circles seen in perspective, so intangible that we hardly notice them. Mary is a delicate and aristocratic young lady elegantly dressed in the contemporary fashion. The convincingly chubby bambino is doing what any normal baby would do; looking at his mother and

65

reaching out his arms to her. But mother is not about to receive her baby, she is lost in contemplation and seems to be gazing at the nearest little angel who is supporting the child. Now this little "angel" is nothing more or less than a street urchin whose impish grin, looking out of the picture at you, the spectator, seems to demand attention. Here is humanism in painting. Somehow we have entered a real world in which there will be diapers to change, noses to wipe, tears to dry, and laundry to do. But it is a soft and delicate world radiating the confident optimism of the early Renaissance; gone is the agony of a Gothic crucifixion, the transcendent otherness of a Byzantine icon, and the intellectual nit-picking of Scholasticism; when we look at this little angel we are looking directly at humanity. Was the mind of the sixty-year-old monk going back to the time when he begat a baby boy from the loins of a nun? Did little Philip or one of his playmates pose for the little angel? Or for the Christ child?

With Botticelli we come to the high-tide of the first phase of the Renaissance in Florence which we can think of as ending with the death of Lorenzo de'Medici in 1492. An interesting thing about Botticelli is the fact that he lived until 1510 to witness the turmoil and tension of Savonarola's days, the corruption of the papacy under Alexander VI and the depredations wrought by the pope's son Caesar Borgia. It is possible to recognize two phases in Botticelli's work corresponding with these two periods; peace and plenty followed by strife and turmoil. Three of his best known paintings come from the first period; the *Allegory of Spring* (1478), the *Madonna of the Magnificent* (1483), and the *Birth of Venus* (1485). Both the "Primavera" and the painting vulgarily known as "Venus on the Half Shell" are a radical departure from the subject matter of previous paintings. Here we have a rather esoteric imagery drawn from classical mythology. The sophisticated viewer *might* see a spiritual allegory of perfect womanhood and divine fecundity, but it is also possible to forget the allegory and derive sensual pleasure from langorous and graceful female nudes. (Plate No. 20, Plate No. 21, Plate No. 22)

We see the same grace and beauty in the *Madonna of the*

Magnificent. The angels are no longer imps or stereotyped little people with artificial wings. They have grown up into the wistful moodiness of late adolescence, radiating feminine charm; one can find them today with almost the same hairstyling and costume sitting in the back row of a psychology lecture at Smith, Bennington, or Bryn Mawr.

In these paintings there is no agony or suffering, the Son of Man is far away, Satan is on vacation, and the world is joyously peaceful as man fulfills himself in many ways.

But there were clouds just under the horizon. With the death of Lorenzo (in the year that Columbus discovered America) an underground opposition bobbed to the surface, a full blown militant ANTI-SATAN response under the spiritual leadership of the mad monk Savonarola who was to the Medici what Rasputin was to the Romanovs. A puritan mystic who saw the Devil lurking in all worldly "vanities," Savanorola attracted huge crowds in the cathedral to hear his fiery, apocalyptic sermons. He sponsored the famous bonfire of vanities in which, among other things, a number of books and works of art were fed to the flames. He believed that the old republic must be restored and that Florence needed no other Head of State than Christ the King.

The French selected this particular time to invade Italy, all of the key Florentine defense positions were surrendered in a series of diplomatic blunders, and it seemed as if the brief Renaissance was over. In the years to come Florence was to be a pawn in the game of European power politics.

In the year that Savanorola came to power Botticelli painted the *Calumny of Apollo* in which we see an allegorical episode full of violence and tension accented by the fixed perspective and formality of the architectural background. (Plate No. 23) There is a framework of good order like a stage, but in this frame and on this stage horrible things are happening. Toward the end of his life, when things were going from bad to worse, Botticelli painted the realistically grim *Deposition* in which the limp and very dead body of Christ is being prepared for burial. (Plate No. 24) There are no haloes, no angels, and no suggestion of an impending resurrection.

God is dead. This is stark tragedy, the end of the line, the ultimate horror. How diffierent this is from the *Allegory of Spring* and the *Birth of Venus*.

If we consider humanism as a belief in man who is doing things in the real world and cultural products such as paintings as responses, we find that early Renaissance belief and action logically support each other. "All of the arts of the mind and hand" that Guicciardini speaks about as part of Lorenzo the Magnificent's Florence go together and make sense. There is consistency among the various elements of the cognitive structure. There is a Gestalt. There is balance and symmetry, order and optimism. Man is in the center of the stage, picking up where the ancient world had left off, building, creating, and fulfilling himself. "The city enjoyed perfect peace, the citizens were united and in harmony, and the government so powerful that no one dared oppose it."

But presently the stage becomes slippery with blood and optimism turns into cynical disillusionment. With the death of the Great Patron the government falls apart, the Savonarola republic is unsuccessful, foreign armies invade the land, and it seems that Man is flunking the course; He no longer justifies the confidence which humanism placed in Him. The Renaissance is over in Florence and dissonance is again on the rise.

This is a microcosm, a single little biased sample. Obviously, the Renaissance is not ended because we find it spreading over Europe to flower in the England of Shakespeare a good hundred years later. The ways in which people came alive and reawakened differ in detail but have the same general pattern. For example, out of the chaos of the War of the Roses comes the strength of Tudor England and the relative security under Elizabeth who was a Great Patron. Time marched on and presently we find a Savonarola-like figure in the person of Oliver Cromwell, the puritan who liked to smash stained glass windows.

REFERENCES

1. Guicciardini, *History of Italy and History of Florence*. Washington Square Press. 1964. Tr. Cecil Grayson, pp. 1, 4, 5.

CHAPTER VIII

Mannerism

We have taken a brief look at the fall of Rome, now we will turn our attention to another depressing spectacle, the decline and fall of the Renaissance. We will continue focusing on Italy as being prototypical.

In 1492 (remember the date?) a Spaniard, Cardinal Rodrigo Borgia, ascended the papal throne as Alexander VI. The name of Borgia is justly associated with fraud and force, with trickery and murder. While still a cardinal, the future pope had fathered at least four children, the two best known to us being the infamous Caesar and Lucrezia of poisoning fame. Alexander achieved his election through threats, blackmail, and the most scandalous sort of open bribery. Once on the throne he proceeded to consolidate his authority by appointing his children to important positions, giving them large estates, and transforming the ancient and Holy City of Rome into a papal fortress, the capital of a state completely preoccupied with worldly and temporal affairs and ruled by the Borgia family. The papal treasury was maintained by simony, extortion, and the sale of indulgences. When Alexander died in 1503 there was not much doubt in anyone's mind but that he went directly to Hell. Fortunately for the papacy, Caesar Borgia was laid up on a sick bed at the time. There is good evidence that he intended to have himself elected the next pope. Burckhardt says: "In pursuing such an hypothesis the imagination loses itself in an abyss."[1]

During Medici rule in Florence, chiefly due to the political sagacity of Lorenzo, the Italian states had enjoyed relative peace among themselves and freedom from foreign interference. Now, two years after his death, the French invaded Italy and swarmed south as far as Naples virtually unopposed. The Kings of Naples were Spaniards, so shortly a Spanish army arrived to fight the French and Italy became the theatre of war between two great contending European powers.

In 1503, the year that Alexander VI died, Naples was annexed to the Spanish crown and in 1519 the King of Spain inherited the vast Holy Roman Empire and, as Charles V, became the world's most powerful ruler, except in the eyes of the King of France who visualized himself in that role. The fighting continued and the principal losers were the Italians. In various coalitions, which were continually dissolving and reforming, they fought against the French, against the Empire, and against each other. There were intrigues, betrayals, treacheries, poisonings, and assassinations; the fact of naked power was the only reality.

This was the ground against which a certain Renaissance man, Niccolo Machiavelli (1469-1517) was a minor figure, though today, the whole age is named after him. He is known for one of his shortest and least scholarly works, and like Ravel, who was sorry that he ever wrote *Bolero*, Machiavelli was probably sorry that he ever wrote *The Prince*. The able historian and political scientist who spent so much time and energy on his *Discourses on the First Ten Books of Livy*, sat down one weekend and dashed off a little do-it-yourself handbook on how to be a successful ruler. *The Prince* may have been written in a fit of paranoia or pique or it may have been written with tongue in cheek, in any event, this is the little pamphlet which gave the author's name to the age in which he lived; the "age of Machiavelli." Here are some of his observations:

(on foreign policy)

No one should ever submit to an evil for the sake of avoiding war, for war is never avoided, but is only deferred to one's disadvantage. (p. 26)

70

(on how to treat a conquered democracy)

And whoever becomes master of a city that has been accustomed to liberty, and does not destroy that city, must himself expect to be ruined. For they will always resort to rebellion in the name of liberty and their ancient institutions. (p. 30)

(on how a prophet must be backed up by force)

All prophets who came with arms in hand were successful, while those who were not armed were ruined. A prophet should be prepared, in case the people will not believe him any more, to be able by force to compel the people to that belief. (pp. 33-34)

(on keeping promises)

A sagacious prince then cannot and should not fulfill his pledges when their observance is contrary to his interest. (p. 86)

(Machiavelli as a psychologist)

Cruelties should be committed all at once, as in that way each separate one is felt less—benefits, on the other hand, should be conferred one at a time, for in that way they will be more appreciated. (p. 48)

But the prince should provide rewards—and besides this, he should at suitable periods, amuse his people with festivities and spectacles.[2] (p. 110)

Here is a view of man quite different from the humanistic ideal with its concern for moral and ethical problems and its love for freedom of thought. However, for those who were engaged in the political business of the day, being a "Machiavellian" tended to reduce dissonance because they could both believe in *and* practice ruthless opportunitism. There is no inconsistency in practicing what you preach. There is "No Dissonance for Machiavellians."[3]

But dissonance must have been high indeed for such people as Erasmus, Michelangelo, and Martin Luther, and the many others who could not rationalize the evils in the world about them. Look at the tortured humanity in Michelangelo's *Last Judgment* and Luther's preoccupation with sin and guilt. On October 31, 1517, Luther, an obscure young professor of theology, posted 95 theses attacking indulgences on the door of the Castle Church at Wittenburg.

The last thing from his mind that day was to start a revolution or found a new religion; an accepted way to make a protest was to write a paper and post it somewhere. There was no unlawful assembly, no windows were broken, no carts were overturned, and no one was wounded by a bolt from a crossbow. At that particular point in history it would appear that the pen was mightier than the sword, though in the years to come many swords would be drawn.

But Luther dipped his pen in vitriol and before long things began to happen. Planted in a soil rich with dissonance, the original protest against abuses quickly became a changed belief in the nature of man and his relationship to God. Man was (obviously) totally evil and corrupt; he could perform no work, engage in no action of his own volition which would justify himself before God; only by his faith could he be saved, salvation was by faith alone.

Both Luther and Machiavelli were motivated by dissonance arising from inconsistencies between the humanistic faith in man and the things which men were actually doing. Both proclaimed a changed belief in the direction of consonance; man *was* evil and sinful (Luther); he *was* a ruthless opportunist (Machiavelli). Perhaps the difference is chiefly semantic. The real difference between the two men lay in the behavior they recommended; to Luther, Faith in God was a mystical state-of-affairs harking back to the early church; St. Paul and St. Augustine. To Machiavelli, salvation was by *virtue;* an intangible something within the individual; elan, morale, spirit, ambition, the need for achievement. Machiavelli was slightly, very slightly, more of a humanist than Luther.

The real world during the age of Machiavelli was the world of Caesar Borgia and his father the pope. It is recorded that Alexander VI had his mistress pose for a painting of the Virgin Mary which hung over the door of the papal apartments.

As a reaction to such vicious evil the next few papal elections produced Vicars of Christ who were not such obvious representatives of the Devil. They were worldly and ambitious but also great gentlemen, patrons of the arts in the best humanist tradition and sufficiently orthodox in their theology to satisfy the scrupulous.

Julius II, pope from 1503 to 1513, was the nephew of a previous pope and had considerable insight into the machinations and skulduggeries of the Roman political morass. He enriched the Church by military and diplomatic maneuvering rather than through the sale of ecclesiastical offices and indulgences. He wished to perpetuate the glories of his reign and decided upon the complete reconstruction of St. Peter's cathedral and the Vatican as his perpetual memorial. Unwilling to live in the apartments of his hated predecessor (with a portrait of a papal mistress as the Virgin Mary) he brought the young Raphael from Florence to decorate his new living quarters. Michelangelo was set to work decorating the Sistine Chapel.

His successor, Giovanni de'Medici, was the famous Leo X. A son of Lorenzo the Magnificent and, like his father, a patron of the arts, he pressed ahead with the work on St. Peter's. He retained the services of Raphael and made him chief architect of the project in 1514. Several years later Raphael painted his famous portrait of *Pope Leo X with His Nephews*. (Plate No. 25)

The one looking over his right shoulder was actually his illegitimate first cousin, Cardinal Guilio de'Medici, later to become Pope Clement VII. It would seem that the Medici family were making the grade.

Leo can be legitimately thought of as a fabulous character. At one time he created 39 new cardinals which served the dual purpose of bringing in a huge sum of money and surrounding him with grateful dependents. Encouraged by Machiavelli he labored on a grand scheme to unify Italy under the rule of his family; this fell through.

Needing more money, he proclaimed the Indulgence of 1515-1517, ostensibly for the building of St. Peter's, while actually much of the income was being used for a number of complex political maneuvers.

Now the idea of an indulgence was not new. It was predicted upon the notion of the "Treasury of the Church"; all of the sanctity and merit deriving from the sacrifice of Saints and Martyrs in the past was on deposit in some sort of heavenly bank with the pope as chief loan officer. They had done such heroic penance that during later generations, if one were truly repentant of sin but was unable to do penance, he could have his penance remitted by appropriating some of that which was stored up. For example, during the Middle Ages if a person confessed to a serious sin and was told that as penance he must go on a pilgrimage, he might be permitted to *substitute* a money offering for some worthy cause in lieu of the pilgrimage which was inconvenient or impractical. Sometimes they were indeed inconvenient; recall how, in 1077 the emperor, Henry IV made his famous trip to Canossa where he stood barefooted in the snow for three days before the pope would even hear his confession. Presumably Henry would much rather have bought an indulgence.

Now, however, there was none of the grand drama of such heroic exploits. Things had degenerated to a level of such petty meanness that indulgence salesmen set out from Rome armed with bundles of signed papers (blank checks) which could be bought by anyone. You simply had your name filled in at the top.

This was the particular situation which set Martin Luther to write his theses.

In 1520 Pope Leo excommunicated this stubborn German because he was attacking, not only indulgences, but the papacy and the entire apparatus of the church.

Leo died the next year to be succeeded by a Dutchman, Adrian IV, who threw Rome into a frenzy by his bold suggestion that serious reforms were in order. All was returned to the *status quo* however, as Adrian died within a year. He was followed by the next Medici pope, the bastard of Lorenzo the Magnificent's brother, who became Clement VII. Even in the Rome of 1523 this was a bit of a scandal.

Clement spent most of his time in vacillating diplomatic blunders, backing first one side then the other in the bloody struggle between France and Spain which was now the most effective part of that Empire which, as has been pointed out, was neither Roman nor Holy. In Rome, graft, corruption, bribery, and the most vicious and immoral practices continued unabated. Jacob Burckhardt tells us that "Under Clement VII the whole horizon of Rome was filled with vapors which make the last months of summer so deadly— The pope was no less detested at home than abroad— Thoughtful people were filled with anxiety, hermits appeared on the streets and squares of Rome, foretelling the fate of Italy and of the world, and calling the pope by the name of Antichrist."[4]

In 1527 the Christian army of the Holy Roman Emperor Charles V, unpaid and in need of provisions, invested the Holy City and suddenly became an uncontrolled, bloodthirsty mob, screaming through the streets intent upon rape, murder, and plunder. Looting and destruction knew no bounds. The pope barely escaped with his life and was subsequently held for ransom. With the Sack of Rome the Renaissance came to an end in that city and we find a dispersion of scholars and artists; many went to Venice, others to France, and some wandered neurotically about in search of security and patronage.

This is the background against which we find the emergence of a new style in the arts. It has come to be known as Mannerism.

The word itself does not tell us anything; it simply means "painting in a certain manner," but before the sixteenth century was out the "manner" had spread to all the arts and had infected all of Europe arriving, as usual, later than elsewhere in England with John Donne and some of Shakespeare's "dark" plays.

Mannerism is marked by tension, dissonance, disproportion, imbalance, ambiguity, and instability. One finds great technical virtuosity in the service of scepticism, cynicism, and irony.

Look once more at the painting by Fra Filippo Lippi and the early Botticellies, those painted before the days of Savanarola. (Plate No. 19, 20, 21, 22)

They seem to radiate a breath of life, there is joy and optimism. Now we begin a trend in another direction. Andrea del Sarto (1486-1531) represents the border-line between high Renaissance and that which was to come.

In 1517, the year of Luther's protest, he painted the *Madonna of the Harpies*. (Plate No. 26)

Here we see beautifully proportioned figures painted with an impeccable technique, yet they occupy very shallow space and are not doing anything. It is as if a group of statues had briefly come to life. Symmetry and balance are there, but it is of the sort one associates with inanimate objects. There is an atmosphere of quiet, introspective sadness, a mute appeal for the spectator to join the Holy Mother in the contemplation of some incomprehensible mystery. As with Luther, salvation is to come by faith alone. There is a return to Gothic dualism; the characters here are from another world.

Parmigianino (1503-1540) was one of those who fled from the Sack of Rome and spent the rest of his short life in neurotic wandering. At the time of his death, under tragic circumstances, he was working on his most celebrated painting, known to us as the *Madonna of the Long Neck*. (Plate No. 27)

This is a milestone in the development of mannerism. Mary has a long neck; she also has tapering, graceful fingers, long beyond any possible representation of reality. Her pose is as artificial as one to be found in a fashion magazine today. Is she standing, sitting, leaning, or about to slide off some invisible pedestal? Clearly the naked baby is about to slide off her lap. He looks ill. The "angels" who are all packed together in the left foreground look like a bevy of junior bridesmaids, except for the one nearest to us whose seductively naked leg tends to create a boudoir atmosphere. Mannerism used nakedness for its shock value; look again at Mary's costume; the velvet cloak is falling off her shoulders to reveal a thinly veiled, firm, round breast with the nipple outline clearly visible. Is this the Mother of God?

Mannerism used mocking elegance in poses of the most contrived gracefulness. It also used gross disproportions between figure and ground. What sort of space exists between the packed-in foreground characters and the limitless distance in the right of the picture? What is the role of the ridiculously small "prophet" in the lower right hand corner? Why the billowing drapes in the upper left hand corner?

Venetian mannerism reached its peak with Tintoretto (1518-1594). The most irrational sort of space distortion is found in his *Presentation of the Virgin* painted about 1551. (Plate No. 28) Mary, pictured as a little girl, is climbing a vast set of marble steps, a construction beyond the scope of any builder or architect of any age. She is confronted by the High Priest; high indeed, he looks about fifteen feet tall. The foreground figures have assumed strange artificial poses, especially the old man, lower left, who is overresponding to the situation. The overall effect is of tension and dissonance. This was painted during the years in which the newly founded Jesuit Order was leading the counter-reformation, years of activity for the Holy Inquisition.

The end of the Renaissance is dominated by the towering genius of Michelangelo (1475-1564). His life and work is well presented in the title *The Agony and the Ecstasy*.[5] Nurtured in the household of Lorenzo de'Medici, he spent his long life moving between Florence and Rome as sculptor, architect, and painter; serving the popes, serving the Medici, fighting against both, and fighting against himself. We have spoken of the tortured humanity of his *Last Judgment* painted behind the altar of the Sistine Chapel. (Plate No. 29) After six years of work this was completed in 1541, twenty-nine years after he had completed the ceiling. Some of the events taking place between the execution of these two frescoes were the start of the Reformation, the struggle for the possession of Italy, and the sack of Rome; they should be compared with this in mind. Aside from the difference in subject matter, the *Last Judgment* is very different from the ceiling. Christ is the righteous, angry judge; the time for clemency is gone forever and nothing now remains but execution. Saints and martyrs crowd about demanding justice which the God of wrath and vengence now dispenses. Have we ever seen before a *mesomorphic* Christ with bulging, rippling muscles, without a beard or halo or a tear upon His cheek? The awful naked truth is now revealed and evil men are driven down into the pit that they themselves have dug. There are others who go soaring upward toward the light. Each resurrected body clothes a soul who knows his fate. (Plate No. 30)

The tensions and distortions of mannerism reach a climax with El Greco (1541-1614). Born in Crete, he moved to Venice, then to Rome, and then to Spain, where all of his great works were painted. Long twisted swirling forms, thin acid colors, exaggerated postures, enigmatic expressions, all combine to make us wonder what sort of world the artist is leading us into. We seem to have returned to a Gothic world where dissonance is high and things do not reasonably fit together.

In the *Baptism of Christ,* painted during his maturity (1596-1600) El Greco echoes the moving, twisting forms of Michelangelo. (Plate No. 31) Naked, save for a loincloth, the virile muscular body of Jesus bends toward his cousin John, half hidden in the shadows. Yet he is not a supplicant and there is no self-surrender here; this is not a suffering servant or a man of sorrows, neither is this a supernatural Son of Man coming in the clouds of heaven, this is the spirit and body of a fighter poised for action. He is not being sent by John, whose action seems irrelevant, but by God, His Father, and the central "person" in the drama is the Holy Ghost who is descending in the form of a dove. We feel that when this dove lights upon his shoulder he will turn toward us for combat and he will be a mighty adversary. He is being sent into the world to fight.

We are on the threshold of a breakthrough and at the moment all is chaos. The heavens above are in disrupted turmoil, the earth below awaits in desperate expectation. This is the final effort, an ultimate thrust which leads irrevocably to the last judgment.

The cultural products which we categorize as mannerist are responses made in times of doubt and fear, of troubled conscience, and high dissonance, of inconsistencies between belief and action. When Hamlet tells us there is something rotten in the state of Denmark, he is speaking of the sickness of the world in which he lives. Western culture was ready for a change.

REFERENCES

1. Burckhardt, J. *The Civilization of the Renaissance in Italy. Op. cit.*, p. 133.
2. Machiavelli, N., *The Prince*. Airmont, 1965. Tr. C. E. Detmold.
   p. 26
   p. 30
   pp. 33-34
   p. 86
   p. 48
   p. 110
3. Gies, Florence; Bogart, Karen; Levy, Marguerite. "No dissonance for Machiavellians": paper read before the New England Psychological Association; Boston, 1967.

CHAPTER IX

The Need for Order

Speaking of mannerism Wylie Sypher (1955) says that:

When we try to date this phase of instability in the arts, we find that mannerism appears hard upon the high-Renaissance as a sign of irresolution, a movement deprived of a sense of security, equilibrium, unity, and proportion expressed in Renaissance style; it comes while the energies of the counter-reformation are being rallied at the Council of Trent, presently to burst into full baroque splendor.[1]

We have taken a brief look at mannerist disproportion and tension which is to presently burst into the full splendor of the baroque response described by scholars as having dignity and grandeur, balance and symmetry, pomp and circumstance, massiveness, formality, and good order. Perhaps the best way to evaluate this is to continue looking at some late mannerist responses and compare them with the emerging baroque style. The change here was slower and more diffuse than the sudden outburst of the Renaissance in Florence. We will present Sir Isaac Newton as a key figure in the developing baroque Gestalt.

For example, compare John Donne (1573-1631) who died eleven years before Newton was born with Joseph Addison (1672-1719) who was thirty years younger than Newton. Both of them wrote poems about the sun. Donne's *The Sun Rising* starts out with:

Busy old fool, unruly sun,
Why dost thou thus

Through windows and through curtains call on us?
He ends the poem by saying:

Shine here to us, and thou art everywhere;
This bed thy center is, these walls thy sphere.[2]

Paraphrasing and digesting into modern prose we find that
Donne's message is:

The sun is an unruly old fool who peeks through windows.

His chief duties are to get schoolboys and apprentices
out of bed.

But love knows no season; the time of day or month of
the year don't matter.

The rays of the sun are strong and respected, but I can
turn them off simply by closing my eyes.

If you ask where the Kings of the Earth were yesterday,
I will tell you that they were all together in the same bed.

I am like a prince because I am a dilettante.

Honor and wealth are illusions.

You, the sun, are not as happy as we are because you
are old and need your comforts.

Your only duty is to warm the world, and you do this
when you warm us.

We are the center of the universe.

This is self-centered, subjective, cynical, and obscure to
the point that it must be read several times to get the mes-

sage, and then one wonders whether or not there is a still deeper layer of meaning. Does the sun represent an older generation whose values are no longer relevant to modern needs? Is the poet taking a poke at authority figures? Is he telling us to drop out of the rat race and stay in bed? It is almost as ambiguous as a projective test item; we can read our own needs and frustrations into it.

Compare this with Addison's *The Spacious Firmament on High* which starts out by informing us that:

> The unwearied sun, from day to day,
> Does his Creator's power display,
> And publishes to every land
> The work of an Almighty hand.[3]

The poem jingles along in perfect harmony and order. The message is completely obvious; the heavens declare the glory of God, His power and His majesty, and absolutely nothing else. This is very safe. We might say that it is *petit bourgeois* baroque. It has balance, symmetry, formality, and order, but it lacks the full splendor found in the mature Milton or the sumptuous elegance of Dryden. It is about as exciting as a split-level ranch house.

Shakespeare's later plays are mannerist; men and women do monstrous things and there is something sick about the world of Lear and Hamlet. Milton was born the year in which *King Lear* was written (1608) and two generations after Shakespeare's death completed *Paradise Lost,* rich in its abundance of gigantic spectacle with thundering voices, stupendous vistas, and exaggerated superlative. Let's make a brief comparison.

In *King Lear,* Act I, Scene II, Gloucester may have been speaking of the world in which the play-goers were living when he says:

> These late eclipses of the sun and moon portent no good to us. . . . Love cools, friendship falls off, brothers divide, in cities—mutinies; in countries—discord; in palaces—

83

treason; and the bond is cracked 'twixt son and father.
. . . We have seen the best of our time; . . . all ruinous
disorders follow us disquietly to our graves.[4]

This has a disquieting contemporary ring; disorder in the
cities, disloyalty to the government, a generation gap—everything is going to the dogs.

On the other hand with the baroque response of *Paradise
Lost*, Milton gives us an heroic epic of gigantic proportions
dealing with the cosmic themes of heaven and hell; the creation and fall of man. We hear the voices of God and of His
Son, of angels in the heavenly hierarchy and long speeches
by the central figure of the drama who is Satan. But it is a
world in which good triumphs over evil in an inexorable, pre-
ordained fashion. Order is created out of chaos. In one passage
Milton has Adam and Eve start the day with a prayer which
begins:

> These are thy glorious works, Parent of good,
> Almighty, thine universal frame,
> Thus wondrous fair; thyself how wondrous then!
> Unspeakable, who sitt'st above these heavens
> To us invisible, or dimly seen
> In these thy lowest works, yet these declare
> Thy goodness beyond thought, and power divine.
> Speak, yet who best can tell, ye sons of light,
> Angels, for ye behold him, and with songs
> And choral symphonies, day without night,
> Circle his throne rejoicing, ye in heaven,
> On Earth join, all ye creatures, to extol
> Him first, him last, him midst, and without end.[5]

The "prayer" continues for another 43 lines during which
the Sun sounds the praise of God, the moon and fixed stars
chime in, and the five (sic) planets (wandering fires) move in
a mystic dance, praising the Creator. Presently Air, Mists,
Winds, Fountains, Birds, and Fish all join in the hymn of
praise and hail the universal Lord.

Time and again Milton refers to divine manifestations
and attributes as "unspeakable" and then goes on to speak

about them at great length. Unlike Addison, the poem does *not* jingle along, it plods through page after page of metaphor and simile which the modern reader finds a crashing bore. It is well-ordered, in the same way that the bureaucracy at City Hall is ordered, one may spend all afternoon walking down dusty corridors before finding the person one wished to see, and then he is likely to turn out to be a pompous ass. If there is any tension, it is likely to be the tension of frustration. Was there something baroque and Miltonesque about the Russia of, say, the 1930's when people would stand in line for a hundred grams of butter only to find that it was rancid when they got their little package home many hours later; where the GLORY OF THE PARENT OF GOOD (Stalin) was proclaimed from posters on every wall; where art was formalized; where there were no demonstrations in the streets because no one dared to demonstrate; where there was "good order"; where there was no sense of humor.

Let us return to El Greco and see whether we can discover a bit of sly wit. The painting, the *Burial of Count Orgaz* done in 1586 is rather different from his *Baptism of Christ*. (Plate No. 32)

This illustrates a medieval legend about two saints who miraculously appeared to assist at the funeral of a slain military hero noted for his piety. No attempt has been made to place the scene in its historical context; the saints are dressed in the full vestments appropriate to one of the greater festivals of the church and the count's body is encased in richly decorated armor. The three central figures are painted in flowing colors sharply contrasting with the somber black of the row of spectators, a group of noble gentlemen in the court costume of Phillip II. Their expressions range from bored introspection to polite disinterest. The upper half of the painting is occupied by a heavenly vision of swirling, twisted forms and weirdly lit cloud formations within which appear clusters of semi-detached cherub heads. There is no unity between the legend being re-enacted in modern dress, the detached observers representing the contemporary power structure, and the disturbance going on in heaven. It is fun to look for hidden

85

and imbedded figures in El Greco, there are a number of them in his *Storm Over Toledo,* in this painting one can "see" all sorts of things in the clouds. Look carefully at the angel directly in the middle of the picture. What is he holding in his right hand? Is it an infant, an embryo, or what? Perhaps it is the soul of Court Orgaz being assisted to heaven. This is the empire of Spain where the Holy Inquisition was active, where gold was pouring in to upset the economy, and where the Armada was being fitted out to sail against England. It was a land of vivid contrasts, the country of El Greco's contemporary Cervantes (1547-1616) who could conjure up an old man going about tilting at windmills. Does Don Quixote have anything in common with the gentlemen spectators at this burial? Both Cervantes and El Greco have a subtle, sophisticated, and wry sense of humor completely lacking in Milton's baroque grandeur.

How different El Greco's "Burial" is from another funeral scene, *Landscape with the Burial of Phocion* painted in 1648 by Nicholas Poussin. This illustrates the classical aspect of baroque, allusions made to antiquity, to the world of ancient Rome which was thought of as being imbued with all the sterling virtues of stoicism, restraint, law, and order. (Plate No. 33) There is a restrained grandeur in the well-ordered clarity of Poussin's idealized landscape; it is quiet, austere, and great attention is paid to form and composition. It does not have the flamboyance one associates with many other baroque cultural products. The artist is telling us to be cool, have faith, preserve order, and recreate a better world.

The world of Rubens (1577-1640) is better, but in a different sense. His large canvases are packed with figures showing movement, light, and a gay vitality. They are, at the same time, both sensuous and tender, appealing yet trivial. Consider his *Garden of Love* painted about 1633. (Plate No. 34) Elegant, beautiful people disport themselves in an idealized setting assisted by a gaggle of little cupids. Everyone is relaxed and having a good time. This is not social commentary and Rubens is not being sarcastic, he is simply showing us *his* idea of a well-ordered world.

Plate Number 37: "The Rake's Progress III", Hogarth, Sir John Soane's Museum, London.

Plate Number 38: "Marriage a la Mode", *Breakfast Scene*, Hogarth, National Gallery, London.

Plate Number 39: Etchings, from "The Capriccios", Goya, Prado.
Original plate numbers 20, 23, 63 & 65.

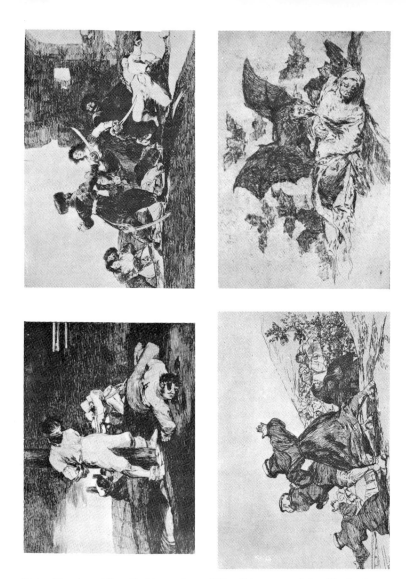

Plate Number 40: Etchings, from "The Disasters of the War", Goya, Prado. Original plate numbers 15, 19, 43 & 72.

Plate Number 41: Photograph, *The Royal Pavilion at Brighton*, John Nash, 1818.

Plate Number 42:   Photograph, *The Houses of Parliament*, London, Sir
Charles Barry, designed 1835.

Plate Number 43: "Moulin de la Galette", Renoir, The Louvre, Paris.

Plate Number 44: "Dance at Bougival", Renoir, Boston Museum of Fine
Arts.

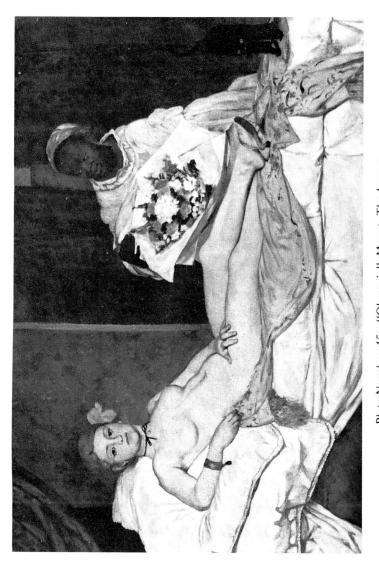

Plate Number 45: "Olympia", Manet, The Louvre.

Plate Number 47: "Study of Rouen Cathedral - Early Morning", Monet, Museum of Fine Arts, Boston.

Plate Number 48: "Isle of the Dead", Bocklin, Metropolitan Museum of Art, New York.

Plate Number 49: "The Bride", Rossetti, Tate Gallery, London.

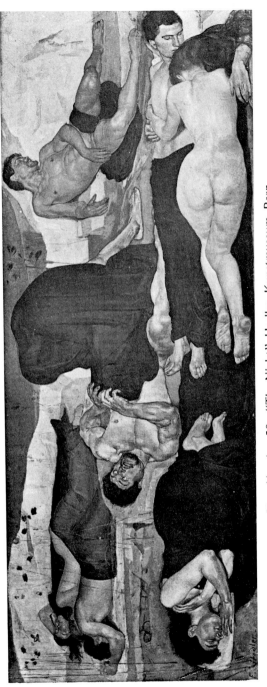

Plate Number 50: "The Night", Hodler, Kunstmuseum, Bern.

Plate Number 46: "Venus of Urbino", Titian, Uffizi.

Plate Number 51: "Melancholy and Mystery of a Street", de Chirico,
Collection of Stanley R. Resor, Greenwich, Conn.

Plate Number 52: "Hide and Seek", Techelitchew, Museum of Modern
Art, New York

Obviously Rubens and Poussin are very different, but for both painters everything is unified and flows together in a harmonious composition and there are no doubts or uncertainties. To this extent they both exemplify the baroque response.

If we must seek a single event out of which this response emerged, it would most likely be the counter-reformation Council of Trent which sat from 1545 to 1563, a happening of eighteen years duration. Sypher (1955) says:

> Thus the Council, which had convened in a climate of mannerist doubt, laid the foundations for a settlement in theology and a reintegration of style in the arts, the baroque acceptance of secular pomp and the sufficiency of the flesh. When the Council had done its work, the arts moved with gathering momentum toward full declarations of power and glory . . .

> The Council of Trent announced its decrees with majestic voice; it did not argue but proclaimed; it brought conviction to the doubter by the very scale of its grandeurs . . .

> The baroque style reaches its decisions through spectacle. . . .

> It is art given to superlatives.[6]

We see this change well illustrated within the confines of one building, St. Peter's in Rome. Michelangelo's fresco of the *Last Judgment* (Plate No. 29) was completed in 1541, before the Council was convened, during the years of doubt and bad conscience. Now within the next hundred years various changes were authorized in the style and construction of the building to culminate in the work of Bernini who designed the stupendous bronze canopy over the high altar and the colonnade forming the piazza in front of the basilica. This epitome of the baroque in architecture points to the greatest monument in Christendom and says— Look here whence

87

flows all of the majesty, might, power, and glory than mortal man can stand— Bernini did with bronze and stone what Milton did with words. (Plate No. 35)

An early response to the dissonance reflected in mannerism was the concerted effort to bolster up the established belief system made by the Jesuits. The *Society of Jesus* was founded in 1540 (the year Parmigianino died, look once more at the *Madonna of the Long Neck*. (Plate No. 27) This rapidly developed into a hard-core army of devoted men dedicated to the propagation of the historic faith. They were trained to present Catholicism on an intellectual level with carefully thought-out reasoning, and Jesuit confessors became experts at resolving problems of conscience, at pointing out the justification of choosing the lesser of two evils, of making quasi-legal decisions as to what sort of good work might be effective in atoning for what particular sort of sin. This process is known as *causistry*, and many times it is simply a sophisticated form of rationalization. The quieting of conscience effects the reduction of dissonance. Causistry was consistent with the baroque response.

Meanwhile, north of the Alps, the belief system was developing in what seemed to be an entirely different direction. In Luther's credo man was saved and justified, not by any good works that he might do, but by his faith alone (p. 72). This was completely inconsistent with causistry, but presently in some Protestant circles we find the development of the doctrine of *election;* certain people were pre-ordained for salvation while others were not. A logical development of this was the thought that God would show favor to His Elect, and what could be more obvious evidence of favor than material success here on earth? Clearly, the enterprising businessman who kept his faith and balanced his books on the black side of the ledger was one of these fortunate people, and if others suffered from his aggressive methods, well, perhaps they were not of the Elect and it was the will of God. Here was a handy way to quiet conscience and reduce dissonance.

Catholic and Protestant views on the problems of conscience were different, but they shared the same baroque frame of reference by rationalizing the sufficiency of the flesh and of things material. Outward manifestations of splendor were appropriate to both as signs of success and symbols of power. Both Jesuit causistry and the Protestant ethic were consistent with the new splendor in the arts; yet it was to be a long time before there would be any peaceful coexistence between the two systems of theology.

The tensions in Germany came to a head in 1618 with the start of the Thirty Years' War. This bloody period in Western Civilization is hard to describe; actually the word *civilization* is hardly appropriate as large areas of central Europe were reduced to the most degraded form of barbarism.

The turmoil started for what were ostensibly political reasons; the vacant throne of Bohemia (now part of Czechoslovakia) was offered to Frederick, Elector of the Palatinate (a district on the upper Rhone) rather than to Ferdinand, the Holy Roman Emperor, who had a more "legitimate" claim. Frederick was a Protestant while Ferdinand was a Hapsburg and a Catholic. When Frederick accepted the crown, an Imperial army was dispatched post haste to correct the situation in Bohemia. Shortly they were joined by a Spanish force detoured from its march to Holland where it was being sent to kill Protestant Dutchmen for the greater glory of God, and before long the Bohemian problem was solved to the satisfaction of constituted authority. A few heads rolled and Frederick fled into exile. The Spaniards continued their march northward through Germany.

But they were not welcome. This situation was not satisfactory to many of the German princes, at least half of whom were Protestant, nor to the masses of people who were predominantly of the new religion. What had started as a political power move rapidly developed into a war of religion with all of the insane passion and illogical paradox associated with that most debasing form of human behavior.

As time went on first one then another of the European powers felt obliged to intervene. Denmark and Sweden could not let the God of Luther down, so first a Danish and then a Swedish army made its appearance. Gustavus Adolphus, defender of the faith (Protestant) and protector of Swedish economic and political hegemony, swept across the country with the most efficient fighting force in Europe. He was hailed as a liberator until one day he was killed in battle leaving his army leaderless.

The senseless fight went on with temporary advantages going to first one side then the other. When it seemed that the Imperial Catholic forces were getting the upper hand we find one of those dissonance producing paradoxes of history where belief and action do not go together and support each other. Cardinal Richelieu, a prince of the Church who was *also* the minister of France, intervened on the Protestant side. Religious and ideological considerations were subservient to the national interests which had run contrary to those of the Empire for so many years. Continuous economic and political rivalry made it impossible for France to accept a victory by Spain and the Empire.

However, court intrigue and international power balances were of minimal concern to the farmers and artisans actually living in Germany at the time. For them the real and terrible fact of existence from day to day, month to month, and year to year, was the presence of armies living off the land; their land from which they must somehow wrest a livelihood.

As Napoleon observed, an army marches on its stomach, and when the supplies from home are exhausted, what is left but to eat the local food? When an army runs out of money and there is no food in the markets, there is nothing left to do except plunder, and this was a major feature of the Thirty Years' War. Of course, in our more enlightened age we can air-lift supplies to our troops who are fighting on some foreign shore to preserve the *status quo,* but in those bad old days it made no difference whether the army was Swedish, Spanish, Bavarian, or Austrian, or whether the countryside was Catholic or Protestant, when an army appeared, any army, the people knew that their livestock would be slaughtered, their grain harvest eaten, their wine drunk, and quite likely, their daughters raped. Armies, like swarms of locust, literally devoured everything in their paths. One strategy of the war was to maneuver an opposing force into an area which had already been despoiled so that the enemy troops would grow so weak from starvation that they could no longer fight. Imagine the condition of the people who lived in such areas!

When peace finally came it was the deathly quiet peace of utter exhaustion. At the outset of the war people might have talked about heroes and liberators, patriots and freedom fighters, a sacred heritage, and the faith of their fathers; but toward the end they were so used up that they could not even conduct a good massacre.

And no problems had been solved. In general, areas which had been Protestant before remained Protestant and the Catholic parts of the country remained Catholic. The European balance of power had not changed significantly. In 1648, the year of the Peace of Westphalia (the year Poussin painted *Landscape with the Burial of Phocion* (Plate No. 33) saw the beginning of a civil war in France which was to last eleven years and the execution of Charles I of England ushering in the period of repression (good order?) under Cromwell.

Yet the baroque response continued to develop during these troubled times. The divergence of the two belief systems was sufficient to perpetuate a war for thirty years; but it was confined to Germany and in that unfortunate country cultural productivity came to a virtual standstill and remained dormant for many years. The level of dissonance had reached an upper limit beyond which it was not stimulating and motivating, only painful and disrupting. One cannot rationalize starvation. However, elsewhere on the continent churches were being built and pictures painted which reflected the need for stability and order, activities directed toward a synthesis in which there would be a consistent pattern among all of the elements of the social cognitive structure.

The year 1660 marked the restoration of the monarchy in England and the founding of the Royal Society dedicated to the furtherance of scientific enterprise, and in France the beginning of Colbert's able ministry under the personal direction of Louis XIV.

Speaking of these times, Bertrand Russell (1945) tells us that:

> The period from 1660 to Rousseau is dominated by recollections of the wars of religion and the civil wars in France and England and Germany. Men were very conscious of the danger of chaos, of the anarchic tendencies of all strong passions, of the importance of safety and the sacrifices necessary to achieve it. Prudence was regarded as the supreme virtue; intellect was valued as the most effective weapon against subversive fanatics; polished manners were praised as a barrier against barbarism. Newton's orderly cosmos, in which the planets unchangingly revolve about the sun in law-abiding orbits became an imaginative symbol of good government. Restraint in the expression of passion was the chief aim of education and the surest mark of a gentleman.[7]

Newton's orderly cosmos was presented to the world in 1687 with the publication of his *Principia* which demonstrated how a single mathematical principle could explain such diverse phenomena as the movement of planets and the rise and fall of tides. Mannerism had been a long time in dying and baroque responses had been going on for well over a hundred years, but now we have reached the top of a mountain and from here all the water is shed down one side in a majestic, smoothly flowing river whose banks are carefully tended to prevent floods and washouts. The seventeenth century "Age of Reason" was to shortly become the eighteenth century "Age of Enlightenment"; the goddess of Reason had enlightened the world and ushered in a millenium described in the little doggerel:

> Nature and Nature's Laws lay hid in Night:
> God said, Let Newton be! And all was Light.[8]

In France the light was seen to be incarnate in the person of a king. Louis XIV became the center of a system in which courtiers revolved in law abiding orbits. The palace at Versailles, the miles of formal gardens, the stage productions, operas, and ballets, the grand levees, and official ceremonial, all combined in harmony to make a complete baroque Gestalt. Now Ruben's *Garden of Love* seemed to be for real. The system did not last, but for a season all things appeared to be in perfect order.

REFERENCES

1. Sypher, W., *Four Stages of Renaissance Style*. Anchor Books, 1955. pp. 104-105.
2. Donne, J. *The Sun Rising. The Standard Book of British and American Verse*. Op. cit. p. 93.
3. Addison, J. *The Spaceous Firmament on High*. Ibid. p. 178.
4. Shakespeare, W. *King Lear*. Act I, Scene II.
5. Milton, J., *Paradise Lost*. Book V, 153-165. Mentor Book, 1961. p. 149.
6. Sypher, W. Op. cit. pp. 180-181.
7. Russell, B., *A History of Western Philosophy*. Simon and Schuster, 1945. p. 677.
8. Pope, A., *Epitaph Intended for Sir Isaac Newton*. (From Bartlett's Quotations)

CHAPTER X

The Need for Elegance

There is a story about an English civil servant who was posted to a remote jungle village. He was the only white man for miles around. Each evening it was his custom to bathe, shave, put on his dinner jacket and sit down to a formal dinner complete with white table cloth and (black) servants. The story may be apocryphal but it serves to illustrate a point in the theory of aristocracy. There was no dissonance in this action; he believed he was superior so he acted superior. A touch of elegance lends a certain feeling of security.

Today we hear a good deal about "upward social mobility through education"; is it possible to conceive of upward social mobility through *elegance?* The servants were required to bathe, shave, and wear clean white uniforms; there was no dissonance for them as long as *they* believed in what they were doing. There is a degree of security in being associated with something which is secure.

Today the civil servant is retired and living on social security (e.g. a small pension) in southern England. The son of one of his former black servants learned to speak English well and was sent to Oxford. Today he is the President of an independent Black Republic which is doing rather well because there is a black civil service available to run the country; elegant people who have been well educated by their former "masters."

So here is an apology for the existence of aristocracy. When one *believes* in good works and then *does* good works

95

there is no inconsistency; no dissonance. Under these happy circumstances there seems to be truth, justice, order, harmony, and a spirit of "Enlightenment."

This was the state-of-affairs which many people believed had been achieved early in the eighteenth century in Europe. The age of Glory had arrived.

Among the first fruits of this new age of glory was John Locke who advanced an elegant theory of knowledge of tremendous scope in his *Essay Concerning Human Understanding* published in 1690.[1] In the fourth edition of 1700 he added a special section on the association of ideas in which he developed the thought, first expressed by Aristotle, that at birth the mind was like a blank slate and that all mental content was acquired as the result of impressions or "writing" on this slate. Locke was an important figure in a line of philosopher-psychologists who became known as English empiricists and later as British associationists, and who attempted to explain thought processes as the mechanical compounding of simple ideas to make more complex ones. Locke refers to "the incomparable Mr. Newton" and evidently feels that the laws governing mental life could be shown to be as orderly as the laws governing the movement of physical bodies. In some places he sounds like a behaviorist, for example in the *Essay* we find him saying:

> Many children, imputing the pain they endured at school to their books they were corrected for, so join those ideas together, that a book becomes their aversion, and they are never reconciled to the study and use of them all their lives after; and thus reading becomes a torment to them, which otherwise possible they might have made the great pleasure of their lives.[2]

One can visualize an English schoolboy standing at attention and being "corrected" with a cane. Clearly, here is a case of pain being associated with book, presumably a previously neutral stimulus, with subsequent avoidance behavior through fear conditioning. It sounds a little bit like "Albert and the White Rat."[3]

Locke represents very late baroque; it is A.N. (after Newton), and all of creation, including the act of creation itself, has been intellectualized and fitted into the mathematical model. Locke's *Essay* lacks the sublime grandeur of Milton and the pomp and circumstance of Louis XIV, but, after all, Locke was neither a poet nor a king. What *Paradise Lost* and the *Essay Concerning Human Understanding* have in common is that they present the reader with a stupendous PLAN of epic proportions in which consequences inevitably follow from antecedent conditions. The difference is that for Milton it's God's plan; for Locke it's Newton's.

One consequence of the lives and works of Copernicus, Galileo, Descartes, Hobbes, Locke, Leibnitz, and Newton was a trend toward atheism. A continuation of Locke's line of thinking ruled out Divine inspiration, messages from angels, and even the idea of free-will. One popular view during the Enlightenment was that God was like a clock-maker who had created the material universe, wound it up, and then departed for duty elsewhere. Under these circumstances neither causistry nor the doctrine of election were particularly relevant and only the most abysmally ignorant peasant would make the SON OF MAN or the ANTI-SATAN response. No, now the heavenly figure was relegated to mythology and it was the MAN IN ALL HIS GLORY response which was the order of the day. Gothic dualism has become materialistic monism. Renaissance man had flunked the course because he had not yet been enlightened by science and mathematics, but *now* we really *know* the answers and there will be no more Machiavellies, no more Inquisitions, and no more Thirty Year Wars. Perhaps this is the *real* Renaissance.

The concept of elegance follows quite naturally from the establishment of a stable social order. It is used today among mathematicians. An elegant proof of a theorem is parsimonious yet complete, it is simple yet sophisticated. The necessary and sufficient conditions for elegance are good order and internal self-consistency. It is likely to be theoretical rather than applied, and we are operating at a high level of abstraction. In modern mathematics the theory of groups is more elegant than,

97

say, the statistical analysis of population trends or I.Q. tests.

In human deportment elegance, for the male, borders on the effeminate without being overly womanly. One may have long or short hair; it may be straight, curly, or waved, but considerable attention has been paid to it; it has been washed, dyed, powdered, tied-up, or festooned with ribbons; usually the services of a barber or hair dresser have been employed. In the matter of dress, today's elegant man sends his suits regularly to be cleaned and pressed, they are of the latest fashion and just ever so slightly original. His linen is spotless and may be edged with lace. He uses cologne and always has a clean handkerchief. His shoes are polished and his socks *never* droop down about his shoe-tops. In conversation he is bright, brittle, and witty, able to bring out the proper *bon mot* at the appropriate moment. He has impeccable table manners and tends to be a gourmet. He is interested in the arts without being a creative artist; he knows a great deal about music but does not play an instrument; he loves sports but does not play football or ski very well. Like the elegant proof in mathematics he is highly abstracted; theoretical rather than applied.

The elegant female is hardly ever married to the elegant male because they can't stand each other. She has all of his attributes but they are raised to the n*th* power, and she tends just the slightest bit toward masculinity. She is aggressive in conversation and very, very intellectual while being beautifully groomed at the same time. She tries very hard not to be a snob even though she is widely read and traveled. She is a patronness of the arts and may preside over a brilliant salon.

Now these are not bad people, they feel well disposed toward others and can't see why the unemployed can't find work and why the poor are so stupid as to be poor. They would like to help and spend a great deal of time in talking about why the times are out of joint. If we could only apply the clean, simple logic of mathematics. Marie Antoinette was a beautiful, elegant person. Should we talk about the legendary LET 'EM EAT CAKE response?

These are the sort of people who we find in charge toward the end of any particular era which has built up a good strong establishment. We speak of Edwardian elegance, that glorious time of country homes, long week-ends, beautiful horses, and fast women coming toward the end of the Victorian era when the Empire was well established. Note that the public servants from the upper classes were dedicated people who were not corrupt grafters. It was a culture that could support opera and ballet even though Albert Edward would rather eat. Edward VII was a far cry from Lorenzo the Magnificent, but he tried hard and wasn't all bad.

Nicholas II wasn't all bad either, he meant well and was a most refined and elegant person. Look at the artistic productivity during his reign.

Some of us remember Franz Joseph II as being an elegant old man. He was a young man once and lived a life of personal tragedy. During his long career he acted as the city manager of Vienna, planning with clear Newtonian logic where the next sewer should be dug and the next hospital built. He was a dedicated person. He had the most beautiful side whiskers in Europe. The opera flourished and the pastry shops produced the most elegant confections.

We could go on and on through history, but our focus at the moment is on the end of baroque, which was a little too ponderous to be elegant, and on an era which has been called Rococo. If there is any date which can be associated with this change it is 1715, the year in which Louis XIV died. The Sun King had become a rather heavy father figure, it seemed as if for years everyone had talked in whispers as they tiptoed through the miles of corridors at Versailles, the city hall of France. The establishment had been achieved, now it was time to introduce a bit of elegance. The baroque had not quite achieved Rubens' *Garden of Love,* maybe it can now be really true.

Look at *A Pilgrimage to Cythera* painted by Antoine Watteau in 1717. A group of bright young people are preparing to embark for home after having spent the day on Cythera, the island of love which was sacred to Venus. (Plate No. 36) There are no suggestions of cleaning up after a vigorous sex orgy, they do not look tired enough for that. Perhaps they have *talked* about love and have done a little discreet necking. Nothing vulgar. The setting looks like theatre scenery. If one were to substitute Norse Gods and Goddesses it would be a nineteenth century production of *Das Rheingold*.

At about the time this painting was exhibited we find an English contemporary of Watteau writing a poem about the dalliance of a young man with two lovely young women named Euphilia and Chloe. He was the diplomat-poet Matthew Prior (1664-1721) who wrote:

> The merchant to secure his treasure,
>   Conveys it in a borrowed name:
> Euphilia serves to grace my measure;
>   But Chloe is my real flame.
>
> My softest verse, my darling lyre,
>   Upon Euphelia's toilet lay;
> When Chloe noted her desire
>   That I should sing, that I should play.
>
> My lyre I tune, my voice I raise;
>   But with my numbers mix my sighs:
> And while I sing Euphelia's praise,
>   I fixe my soul on Chole's eyes.
>
> Fair Chloe blushed: Euphelia frowned:
>   I sung, and gazed: I played and trembled:
> And Venus to the loves around
>   Remarked, how ill we all dissembled.[4]

How easy for us to imagine this activity taking place on Watteau's Cythera.

Another contemporary of the above two gentlemen, and far and away the best Rococo poet, was Alexander Pope (1688-1744) who wrote *The Rape of the Lock* at about this time. If Milton is given to turning in his grave he must have done considerable rotating when this was published. It is a mock-epic in five cantos, not as long as *Paradise Lost*, but it does go on for page after page. It is cosmetic rather than cosmic, sylphs and gnomes take the place of angels and demons, a group of vapid young people replace Adam and Eve. We have Belinda, the heroine who suffers the indignity of having a lock of hair snipped off by her beau, and Clarissa and Cynthia and, yes, we have Chloe. Euphilia does not appear.

In Canto I Belinda drags herself out of bed at noon and sits at her dressing table:

> And now unveiled, the Toilet stands displayed
> Each silver Vase in mystic order laid.
>
> . . . .
>
> This casket India's glowing gems unlocks
> And all Arabia breathes from yonder box.
>
> . . . .
>
> Here files of pins extend their shining rows
> Puffs, Powders, Patches, Bibles, Billets-doux.[5]

(Note that there is a Bible in there somewhere with the love letters and powder puffs.)

We read on and discover that Belinda "to the destruction of mankind, nourished two locks, which graceful hung behind" and that her beau, the Baron "the bright locks admired; he saw, he wished and to the locks aspired."[6] Presently, the scoundrel sneaks up and cuts off one of the locks, whereupon all Hell breaks loose:

> Then flashed the living lightning from her eyes,
> And screams of horror rend th' affrighted skies.
> Not louder shrieks to pitying heaven are cast,
> When husbands, or when lap-dogs breathe their last.[7]

After considerable maneuvering Belinda corners the miscreant and throws a pinch of snuff in his face.

> But this bold Lord with manly strength indeed,
> She with one finger and a thumb subdued:
> Just where the breath of life his nostrils drew,
> A charge of Snuff the wily virgin threw.[8]

The Baron sneezes so hard that the raped lock is blown up to heaven where it becomes a comet. Finis.

Pope may not have been as good a poet as Milton, but he certainly had a better sense of humor and he was much more elegant. This was the age of the wit, the beau, the fop, and that delightful word macaroni. Today we think in terms of pasta, then macaroni was the attribute of a dandy, a swell, a rich bright young man who affected the latest continental fashions. During the American Revolution the British had a song ridiculing the rude and vulgar rebels; it went:

> Yankee Doodle went to town
> Riding on a pony
> Stuck a feather in his cap
> And called it macaroni.

Seventeen seventy-six, the year of "Yankee Doodle," was also the year in which Adam Smith published his *Wealth of Nations* back in the Mother Country. We can place Smith in a line of thinkers which would later include Jeremy Bentham and John Stuart Mill (p. 59). He was a humanistic capitalist. He said that "Every man, as long as he does not violate the laws of justice, is left perfectly free to pursue his own interest in his own way, and to bring both his industry and his capital into competition with those of any other man, or order of men."[9] In the field of economics he produced a system which was as rigorous and self-consistent as Newton's *Principia* and Locke's *Essay*.

But a development was forming in Western culture which was to place a severe strain on Smith's theories; the industrial revolution. In theory man was now in control of his manifest destiny, in practice, as with Renaissance humanism, he was about to flunk the course again.

If there was dissonance between the elegance of court life and Gray's ploughman who plodded his weary way home, how much more dissonance between the Fop, the Wit, and the Beau, and the bleak horrors of a coal mine and an industrial slum. It seemed that the lights of the Englightenment were burning dimmer and that another change was in the air.

REFERENCES

1. Locke, J. *Essay Concerning Human Understanding.* Reprinted in Dennis, W. (Ed.). *Readings in the History of Psychology.* Appleton-Century-Crofts, 1948.
2. Locke, J. Ibid. p. 68.
3. Watson, J. B., and Rayner, Rosalie. Reprinted in Watson, J. B., *Behaviorism*, Phoenix Books, 1959. pp. 159-164. Original article in *Scientific Monthly*, 1921. p. 493.
4. Prior, M., *Song. The Standard Book of British and American Verse. Op. cit.* p. 175.
5. Pope, A. *The Rape of the Lock. Immortal Poems of the English Language. Op. cit.* p. 168.
6. *Ibid.* p. 169.
7. *Ibid.*, pp. 176-177.
8. *Ibid.* p. 184.
9. Smith, A. *The Wealth of Nations.* Quoted in *Encycl. Brit. Op. cit.* Vol. 20. p. 827b.

CHAPTER XI

Neo-Humanism

In Chapter VI humanism was presented as a changing view of the role of humanity; man was seen as fulfilling his destiny and actualizing himself here on earth rather than as a spiritual creature making his way back to heaven, and it was suggested that this changing belief was brought about by the inadequacies of the Gothic system to explain the facts of the real world. In other words, the stimulus conditions were dissonance and inconsistency.

In Chapter VII we took a brief look at the Renaissance and found a time when "all of the arts of the mind and hand" went together in a consistent system of mutual support; an optimistic time of growth and creativity. Then in the next chapter on Mannerism we examined the hypothesis that this period of cynical disillusionment and high dissonance was brought about by the inadequacies of humanism; man's faith in himself did not seem justified, there was need for a new balance, a new order. Presently, "the incomparable Mr. Newton" arrived on the scene and a light shone in the darkness. Like the Renaissance, the enlightenment was a time of creative growth with man occupying the center of the stage.

However, as the eighteenth century wore on it appeared that flaws were developing in this well-ordered world. There were too many people like Pope's Belinda, too many Euphilias and Choles, too many Beaux and Fops, too much macaroni. Look at the social satire in Hogarth's series of paintings, *A Rake's Progress* (1735) (Plate No. 37) *and Marriage a la*

Mode (1745). (Plate No. 38) Engravings of these were immensely popular and sold as rapidly as they could be printed.

Voltaire (1694-1778) visited England in 1726 and stayed for three years; among his friends was Alexander Pope. A circle of intellectuals developed who met at taverns and coffee houses to discuss the problems of the day; there seems to have been an atmosphere of cynicism and disillusionment. During his long life Voltaire was an indefatigable correspondent and a brilliant conversationalist much like his English contemporary Dr. Johnson. The two men did *not* get on well together, perhaps they were too much alike. Voltaire was anti-clerical, anti-orthodox, and anti-establishment, untiring in his defense of those whom he considered unjustly condemned.

In 1733 a certain John Kay invented the flying shuttle. This seems like a completely irrelevant statement. But it is not. It was a *mechanical* device which enabled fewer people to weave more cloth. If it had not been for the Newtonian frame of reference and preoccupation with things mechanical it might not have been developed. It was a product of the Zeitgeist.

Now people could weave faster than threads could be spun, so the next logical development was the *spinning jenny* which could be operated by water power and increased the production of yarn to the point where the weavers could hardly keep up. Naturally enough, next came a power loom.

The social conditions arising from this state-of-affairs are poignantly described by Oliver Goldsmith (1730-1774) in his poem *The Deserted Village* published in 1770. Note that the form and meter is the same as in *The Rape of the Lock* but the approach to the problem is quite different.

He starts out by describing the simple pleasures of country life in his native village as he remembers them from his boyhood:

> The sheltered cot, the cultivated farm,
> The never failing brook, the busy mill,
> The decent church that topped the neighboring hill,
> The hawthorne bush, with seats beneath the shade.[1]

He goes on to describe a pastoral idyll of rustic bliss, sports and games, and dancing on the green. One suspects that Goldsmith is suffering from the "good old days" syndrome but he does paint a most appealing picture of simple, gracious living.

Suddenly he brings us up short, because NOW:

> Sweet smiling village, loveliest of the lawn,
> Thy sports are fled and all thy charms withdrawn;
> Amidst thy bowers and tyrant's hand is seen,
> And desolation saddens all thy green;
> One only master grasps the whole domain,
> And half a tillage stints thy smiling plain;
> No more thy glassy brook reflects the day,
> But choked with sedges works its weedy way;
> Along thy glades, a solitary guest,
> The hollow-sounding bittern guards its nest,
> Amidst thy desert walks the lapwing flies,
> And tries their echoes with unvaried cries.
> Sunk are thy bowers in shapeless ruin all,
> And the long grass o'retops the mouldering wall;
> And, trembling, shrinking from the spoilers hand,
> Far, far away, thy children leave the land.[2]

Here is a picture of desolation, a place "where wealth accumulates and men decay" and where "rural mirth and manners are no more." Economic pressure is forcing people to leave the land, and—"If to the city sped—what waits them there?"

> To see profusion that he must not share;
> To see ten thousand baneful arts combined
> To pamper luxury, and thin mankind;
> To see those joys and sons of pleasure know
> Extorted from his fellow-creatures woe.[3]

The only other alternative that Goldsmith sees is emigration to some horrid, inhospitable foreign shore:

> Those matted woods where birds forget to sing,
> But silent bats in drowsy clusters cling;

Those poisonous fields with rank luxuriance crowned,
Where the dark scorpion gathers death around;
Where at each step the stranger fears to wake
The rattling terrors of the vengeful snake;
Where crouching tigers wait their hapless prey,
And savage men more murderous still than they;
Where oft in whirls the mad tornado flies,
Mingling the ravaged landscape with the skies.[4]

We don't know exactly what bit of geography Goldsmith had in mind that would combine so many horrors: bats, scorpions, rattlesnakes, tigers, and tornadoes, but he certainly does present an unattractive picture; life can't possibly be as pleasant as back home in the smiling English village.

Goldsmith was writing at the beginning of that period in Western culture which has come to be known as the *industrial revolution,* and which was to continue for another seventy-five years. Actually it was more of a development or evolution than a revolution, and it revolved around textiles, iron, coal, steam, the factory system, and a *labor force.* These last two items account for the many deserted villages.

Is there any possible connection between what is going on during the last half of the eighteenth century and Renaissance humanism which was discussed in Chapter VI? Then it was pointed out that humanism tended to be anti-clerical and skeptical and that it focused on the needs and ambitions, joys, and sorrows of man living here in the real world. We then took a peek into the future and explored such notions as *humane* and *humanitarian* and *liberal.* We mentioned such people as Thomas Gray, Jeremy Bentham, and Jean Jacques Rousseau. Now let's pick up where we left off and take a closer look at Rousseau.

In 1761 Rousseau published one of his major works—*The Social Contract, or Principles of Political Right.* He opens chapter one by saying: "Man is born free; and everywhere he is in chains." He believes that "The most ancient of all societies, and the only one that is natural, is the family." All other societies are contrivances born out of expediency and sooner or later they outlive the purpose for which they were formed. Rousseau is preoccupied with the idea of nature, natural conditions, and natural law. For example, slavery is un-natural "Since no man has a natural authority over his fellow"; and "To yield to force is an act of necessity, not of will—at the most an act of prudence. In what sense can it be a duty?" and "To renounce liberty is to renounce being a man, to surrender the rights of humanity and even its duties"; and "The right of conquest has no foundation other than the right of the strongest." He then goes on to discuss various problems connected with sovereignty and the State, which he does *not* see as a "work of art."

Rousseau opens Book II by stating that—"the general will alone can direct the State according to the object for which it was instituted, i.e. the common good"; and that "It is solely on the basis of this common interest that every society should be governed." (At this point the interested reader should compare *The Social Contract* with our own Declaration of Independence, it seems that Rousseau and Jefferson were breathing the same air.)

In the chapter on "The Right of Life and Death" Rousseau states that—"There is not a single ill-doer who could not be turned to some good. The State has no right to put to death, even for the sake of making an example, any one whom it can leave alive without danger." This sounds rather *avant garde* even for today. Another statement which seems appropos to some of today's problems is "the wise legislator does not begin by laying down laws good in themselves, but by investigating the fitness of the people, for which they are destined, to receive them."

In Chapter IV, "The Dark Ages," in connection with the fall of Rome, the question was asked—does sheer bigness contribute to survival? Rousseau has an answer to this, he says—"In every body politic there is a maximum strength which it cannot exceed and which it only loses by increasing in size. Every extension of the social tie means its relaxation; and, generally speaking, a small State is stronger in proportion than a great one." Today one thinks of the Scandinavian countries and perhaps, Switzerland; Rousseau, by the way, was Swiss. These states are *strong* to the extent that there is no crime in the streets, little poverty, and no threat from foreign invasion. They are *weak* to the extent that they are not armed with atomic weapons and are not engaged in international warfare. But let's not get into that. Let's get back to Rousseau who said that "A body politic may be measured in two ways—either by the extent of its territory, or by the number of its people; and there is, between these two measurements, a right relation which makes the State really great. The men make the State, and the territory sustains the men; the right relation therefore, is that the land should suffice for the maintenance of the inhabitants, and that there should be as many inhabitants as the land can maintain." This makes us think of *The Deserted Village,* there *was* a balance between the land and the men living on it, but now the men have moved to the ghettos and slums, how will they be maintained?

It is hard to believe that all of this was written two hundred years ago. We will conclude this section with a few more quotes from Rousseau; viz.

> The more numerous the magistrates, the weaker the government.

> (Machiavelli) professed to teach kings; but it was the people he really taught. His *Prince* is the book of Republicans.

> Governments never change their form except when their energy is exhausted and leaves them too weak to keep what they have.

> If Sparta and Rome perished, what State can hope to endure forever? If we would set up a long-lived form of government, let us not even dream of making it eternal.[5]

This last statement seems to be Rousseau's answer to another of the questions asked in previous chapters—Is any culture immortal?

If Newton's *Principia* (1687) represents the high tide of rational optimism, now, less than a century later, we find that the tide has pretty well gone out leaving a vast expanse of mud-flat in which helpless people were wallowing. These people could be seen dragging chains behind them; not like the chains of Marley's ghost which he had forged himself out of ledgers and money boxes, but chains forged by others from flying shuttles, spinning jennys, and power looms. The new humanism focused on the human condition and saw, with Rousseau, that "Man is born free, yet everywhere he is in chains."

Inconsistencies between the well-ordered Newtonian Enlightenment and the actual facts of human existence were too great and dissonance was once more on the rise. Adam Smith attempted a rational solution to the problem from within the framework of the existing system; Thomas Gray, Robert Burns, Oliver Goldsmith, and others like them with the inner vision of the poet, saw things differently. Rousseau was their philosopher.

During the eighteenth century there was a revival of the SON OF MAN response peculiarly fitted to meet the needs of the times (see Chapter I). The best known names connected with this evangelical revival were Charles and John Wesley. They preached personal holiness, total conversion, and "a desire to flee from the wrath to come and be saved from sin." The Methodists also combined this with the ANTI-SATAN response (see Chapter III). Bands of traveling Methodist lay-preachers worked in prisons, factories, and alms houses. They actually preached in fields and on street corners. There was nothing elegant or rococo about Charles Wesley's hymn:

> Come, Thou long expected Jesus,
> Born to set thy people free;
> From our fears and sins release us;
> Let us find our rest in thee.
>
> Israel's Strength and Consolation,
> Hope of all the earth thou art;

Dear desire of every nation,
Joy of every longing heart.

Born thy people to deliver,
Born a child and yet a King.
Born to reign in us forever,
Now thy gracious Kingdom bring.

By thine own eternal spirit
Rule in all our hearts alone;
By thine all sufficient merit,
Raise us to thy glorious throne.[6]

Conditions are getting so bad that people are looking for a supernatural source of outside help. That is the common people; the intellectuals were atheists.

REFERENCES

1. Goldsmith, O., *The Deserted Village. Immortal Poems of the English Language. Op. cit.* p. 211.
2. *Ibid.,* p. 212
3. *Ibid.,* p. 219.
4. *Ibid.,* p. 220.
5. Rousseau, J. J., *The Social Contract and Discourses. Everyman's Library* 660A, 1950.
6. *The Hymnal of the Protestant Episcopal Church. Op. cit.* Hymn 1, Charles Wesley, 1744.

CHAPTER XII

The Romantic Response

Disordered and illogical conditions of existence create needs for a new and better world in which people can exist reasonably, a world in which things go together and make sense, in which there are consistent relationships between the belief system and the products of the culture, between ethos and style.

We have postulated that social dissonance is high when the belief system, a set of established values, is no longer able to explain or contain the facts of real existence. This dissonance is frequently the cause of group anxiety and a concomitant of group frustration. The Gothic system could not explain the newly emerging conditions of man in the real world, the humanism of the Renaissance could not explain the failures of mankind, and now the well-ordered Newtonian enlightenment could not explain the fact that everywhere men were in chains. Dissonance is high once more, there are too many inconsistencies among the cognitive elements of the social structure.

There are any number of ways in which people can cope with dissonance. One may make the MARY BAKER EDDY response and deny the reality of evil (Chapter III, p. 32), or one may make the ANTI-SATAN response and withdraw to the desert. Other withdrawal responses include insulation, negativism, and taking to alcohol or drugs; inconsistencies don't *seem* so bad if you are drunk. During the eighteenth century gin was cheap and plentiful, the poor man's helper when all else had failed. Tincture of opium (laudanum, not paregoric) was also readily available. These responses did not reduce dissonance, they masked it and made it easier to live with. Still other palliative behaviors are escapes into fantasy or becoming involved with a new religion which offers the SON OF MAN in some form or other. Once having made a decision to proceed in any of these directions, dissonance theory predicts that the individual will perceive all the good things and ignore the bad things resulting from the choice he has made; that is, he will grow stronger in his belief.

More aggressive responses to the anxiety and frustrations of social dissonance run anywhere from heckling the speaker to riot, revolution, and militant nationalism. These are changed actions which will hopefully bring about more equitable and consistent conditions of existence. In other words, if I can't change my belief that slavery is evil, and I find that I own slaves, I can reduce the resulting dissonance by the action of freeing my slaves. But in the dynamics of a group, seeing that my neighbor is exploiting human chattel is dissonant with my having freed my own slaves, so I will try to reduce this group dissonance by fighting to free *his* slaves. Presently we are engaged in a revolution or civil war, with "liberty" as an ideal for which people will fight and die. The new ideal is part of the new belief system which, in turn, is consistent with the new activities of the culture and a new phase in that civilization gets bravely under way, to last for a season until the cycle repeats itself.

In the last chapter we looked at some of the dissonance being generated during the second half of the eighteenth century, one of the responses to this was the Romantic Movement. This was a trend in Western culture, roughly between 1750 and 1850. It was an outlook on life which did not generate a set pattern and technique for doing things which one might call a style. Today we tend to use the word *romantic* as the opposite of *realistic,* and think of the romanticist as a visionary idealist, oblivious to the mundane practicalities of everyday existence. One speaks of the romance of strange and exotic far-off times and places. The word is also frequently used to mean the opposite of *classical,* implying great freedom of action where content is more important than form. There is a distinctly emotional quality to romantic productions. One also finds, in modified form, the SON OF MAN response, but now the heavenly figure is likely to have become a Savior-Hero who will slay dragons and monsters and lead on to ultimate victory. The Hero is a romantic ideal.

The story is told that Beethoven dedicated his great third symphony to Napoleon only to tear up the title page upon hearing that the Champion of Liberty had caused himself to be proclaimed Emperor of the French in 1804. Subsequently, this work was published with the title and motto: "Heroic Symphony, composed to celebrate the memory of a great man."

Goethe wrote of Count Egmont and the liberation of the Netherlands; in 1810 Beethoven composed the overture to the play *Egmont.* Here is the martyrdom of a hero, the turmoil of insurrection, and the triumphal sounds of victory announcing the tyrant's downfall.

Schiller wrote of the hero William Tell in 1804; Rossini composed the opera in 1829 with its famous overture emotionally depicting the forces of liberty arriving on horseback in the nick of time.

The preceding dynastic wars which had used professional armies bred fewer heroes than did revolutions and romantic outbursts of nationalism. The hero became the symbol of hope, the projection from a fantasy world where virtue would be vindicated and evil things destroyed. One's needs, longings, and aspirations might also be projected upon the hero; he could be identified with and believed in.

For the more educated, Rousseau was a sort of intellectual hero. His thinking affected the founding fathers of our country and he was adopted as the "official" philosopher of the French revolution. In 1794 there was a nationalistic insurrection in Poland led by Kosciusko who had served so brilliantly as a volunteer under Washington. In that same year a young French artillery officer named Bonaparte was promoted to general. Two years later, at age twenty-seven, he was leading the victorious Peoples' Army of Liberation against the Reactionary Forces of Repression in his brilliant Italian campaign. To many people, like Beethoven, he became the betrayer of the revolution, but to many more he was the ultimate hero, a charismatic figure capable of inspiring unlimited devotion, the white hot hope of people seeking a new world of personal freedom and logical order.

This new world was badly cut up at the Congress of Vienna in 1815, but the idea of national boundaries consistent with the needs of the people did not perish and in 1822 came the Greek declaration of independence against the Turks which stirred the imagination of many Europeans including George Gordon, Lord Byron, who wrote:

> The isles of Greece, the isles of Greece!
>   Where burning Sappho loved and sung,
> Where grew the arts of war and peace—
>   Where Delos rose and Phoebus sprung!
> Eternal summer gilds them yet,
> But all, except their sun, is set.
> . . . .
>
> The mountains look on Marathon—
>   And Marathon looks on the sea;
> And musing there an hour alone,
>   I dreamed that Greece might still be free;
> For standing on the Persian's grave,
> I could not deem myself a slave.[1]

This is heady stuff, a clarion call to arms and action, quite different from the baroque splendor of Milton, the rococo elegance of Pope, or the plaintive wailing of Goldsmith.

Those who could not get away from home to fight in Greece might follow Byron's Childe Harold on his pilgrimage, sailing off in their imaginations:

> With thee, my bark, I'll swiftly go
>   Altward the foaming brine;
> Nor care what land thou bear'st me to,
>   So not again to mine.

Welcome, welcome, ye dark blue waves
And when you fail my sight,
Welcome ye deserts, and ye caves,
My native land—Good Night.[2]

In 1834 Paris heard the first performance of Berlioz'
Harold in Italy, a symphony which was really a series of
scenes for orchestra and solo viola, the instrument being introduced as a sort of melancholy dreamer in the style of
Byron's hero.

In the romantic ideal the individual artist, poet, or musi-
cian must be a melancholy figure, living in a garret, wearing
an old velvet jacket, eating cold beans, and with his pale,
anxious face framed by long, flowing, unkempt hair. In 1830
Berlioz, in the explanatory preface to his "Fantastic Symphony" wrote:

> A young musician of morbid sensibility and ardent imag-
> ination poisons himself with opium in a fit of amorous
> despair. The narcotic dose, too weak to result in death,
> plunges him into a heavy sleep accompanied by the
> strangest visions, during which his sensations, sentiments,
> and recollections are translated in his sick brain into
> musical thoughts and images.[3]

Clearly, here is a young man having a "bad trip." The
last movement of this work is entitled "Walpurgis Night's
Dream"; Berlioz says:

> He sees himself at the Witches' Sabbath, in the midst
> of a frightful group of ghosts, magicians, and monsters
> of all sorts, who have come together for his obsequies.
> He hears strange noises, groans, ringing laughter, and
> shrieks, to which other shrieks seem to reply.[4]

The romantics were not only preoccupied with the Hero
and the Melancholy Poet, but with Nature in all of her terrible
grandeur. It may be argued that the wild mountain torrents
and pathless forests of romantic fiction were no more realistic

than the artificial drawing-room situations of the baroque and the rococo; but at least they were different. The "Gothic Novel" with its ruined castles complete with ghosts, wizards, monsters, thunderstorms, and aura of forboding, is typical of romantic fiction. Many of these novels and short stories were "psychological." Questions were being asked about human needs, goals, compulsions, frustrations, and tension states. The hero, the dungeon, the premature burial, and the monster were all vehicles for the exploration of man's emotions, passions, and motives. Mary Shelly may not have set out to solve the mind-body problem when she wrote *Frankenstein* in 1818, but she did present the reader with the picture of a creature who had been mechanically constructed, who had a "mind," and whose aggressive behavior was the consequence of his treatment by other people.

But Nature is not always weird and mystical, sometimes She is kindly and sweet. Consider the descriptive titles which head the separate movements of Beethoven's "Pastoral" (sixth) symphony:

1. Awakening of joyful impressions on arriving in the country.
2. Scene by the brook.
3. Merry gathering of country folk.
4. Thunderstorm.
5. Shepherd's song: glad and thankful feelings after the storm.

Here is change in the direction of an idealized state-of-affairs. The listener is projected into a reverie of imaginary experience. To the composer it was a reverie of remembered experience because by 1808, when this work was written, Beethoven's deafness had progressed to the point where he could not hear the shepherd singing or the village band playing for the merry gathering of country-folk.

This symphony is a good example of the individual artist's personal needs interacting with the general needs of the times in which he lived. Earlier in the same year the rousing fifth symphony had been completed with its opening theme of "fate knocking on the door" and its finale of joyous victory. Now with the sixth we lapse into quiet contemplation; even the storm is restrained with most of the thunder heard in the distance. Yet, both of these works bear the indelible stamp of the times in which they were written. Bach could not and would not have produced something as wild and wonderful as the surging opening of the last movement of the *fifth* or used the bassoon with the simple, plaintive melancholy that Beethoven used in the *sixth*. The "Pastoral" isn't even a symphony in the classical sense; both the form and style are different.

When taken as a group, country-folk were given to merry gatherings, bands of Gypsies played "soul music" on violins, and at an appropriate moment, would break out into a "Hungarian Dance." On the other hand, individual members of the rural population might be the pathetic victims of a fate worse than death; the villain wrought his dastardly deeds, but this would set the stage for heroic rescue operations in the last act.

Perhaps the best examples of romantic opera are the works of Carl Maria von Webber (1786-1826). In *Der Freischütz* (1821) we have a Huntsman selling his soul to the Demon Hunter in exchange for seven magic bullets which are guaranteed to always hit the mark. By accident the last mark is the heroine Agatha, and indeed, she is hit, falling quite dead upon the stage (left center). However, at this opportune moment a strange hermit enters from the wings (right rear) and brings her back to life. The Huntsman is chided and sent away.

In Paris Theophile Gautier wrote ". . . the Opera was given over to gnomes, undines, salamanders, nixes, willis, peris—to all that strange and mysterious folk who lend themselves so marvelously to the fantasies of the *maitre de ballet.*"[5] In 1841 Gautier created the ballet *Giselle* which is still in the repertoire of many companies today. The first act is a sequence of colorful peasant scenes but in the second act we really go way out; it seems that "the Willis are abroad." A Willis, by the way, is the ghost of a young woman, who, betrayed by her lover, has died of a broken heart. It is haunting, unearthly, and also absurd.

On a more spiritual level there was the world of William Blake (1757-1837) whose mystical poems and drawings transport one into a bizarre land of otherness. Perhaps this is the same world as that visited by Samuel Taylor Coleridge (1772-1834) where Kubla Khan his stately pleasure dome decreed. A land of miracle and paradox where:

> . . . Kubla heard from far
> Ancestral voices prophesying war!
>   The shadow of the dome of pleasure
>   Floated midway on the waves;
>   Where was heard the mingled measure
>   From the fountain and the caves.
> It was a miracle of rare device,
> A sunny pleasure-dome with caves of ice![6]

Or the hardy dream-voyager might join the Ancient Mariner where:

> The very deep did rot: O Christ!
> That ever this should be!
> Yea, slimy things did crawl with legs
> Upon the slimy sea.
>
> The many men, so beautiful!
> And they all dead did lie:
> And a thousand thousand slimy things
> Lived on; and so did I.[7]

But the slimy things were not in the ghettos and slums, they had been transported into a never-never land where the curse was finally expiated. But in the real world the curse had not been expiated, for behind the facade of fantasy gibbered the idiot faces of poverty, ignorance, and social injustice. There were inconsistencies between the brave new world of revolution and events in the real world.

The real world was portrayed by a man who was considerably ahead of his time, Francisco Jose de Goya (1746-1828). He is best known for two paintings, both alleged to be of the Dutchess of Alba, one with and one without clothing, but for our purpose of particular interest are his two series of etchings; *The Capriccios* (Plate No. 39) and *The Disasters of the War.** (Plate No. 40)

The Capriccios are an allegorical and fantastic series of truly horrible commentaries on the world of evil. We see that plucked chickens have the heads of children (20), and adult human bodies have developed strange and obscene animal heads (63). Mindless idiots gibber away at meaningless tasks (26, 50, 71). Anti-clericalism is evident, we see victims of the Inquisition (23) and vicious cartoons of life in a monastery (49). Throughout the entire series one encounters demons and witches going about their evil business (64, 65, 66, 67). This series is haunted by confusion, violence and useless destructiveness: the atmosphere is one of extreme tension. Aldous Huxley says of them:

> The moral of it all is summed up in the central plate (43) of the Capriccios, in which we see Goya himself, his head on his arms, sprawled across his desk and fitfully sleeping, while the air above is peopled with bats and owls of necromancy and just behind his chair lies an enormous witch's cat, malevolent as only Goya's cats can be, staring at the sleeper with baleful eyes. On the side of the desk are traced the words, "The dream of reason produces monsters."[8]

This group of etchings was published in 1799, the same year in which Coleridge produced the *Ancient Mariner*. ("And a thousand, thousand slimy things lived on; and so did I".)

The slimy things, the horrors and the monsters came to very real life when, in 1808, the French occupied Madrid. In *The Disasters of the War* the 62-year-old Goya shows us, with the most stark realism, man's inhumanity to man. In the previous etchings of 1799 animals and devils had been shown behaving like human beings; now the beasts have be-

---

* *The Complete Etchings of Goya* with a foreword by Aldous Huxley; Crown Publishers, New York, 1943. The numbers I am using refer to the original plate numbers of the etchings.

come incarnate in human flesh and we see humans behaving like animals. There are no grand scenes of colorful military operations, but rather we see men and women before firing squads (15, 26), mothers being raped in front of their small children (11) and over the bodies of their dead husbands (19). From time to time we see representatives of the church (42, 43). Are they spectators or participants? Their position is ambiguous and we cannot tell. Toward the end of this series Goya again returns to the symbolism of witches, demons, and monsters (72, 75, 76). Perhaps his sensitive artist's soul had had all it could take of tortured human bodies and his message was, after all, to be transmitted through symbols.

Goya and Beethoven did not know each other; it is interesting that both men suffered from complete deafness and died within a year of each other.

Here is a completely different sort of social protest from Hogarth's *Rake's Progress* and *Marriage a la Mode* (p. 159). The romanticist's preoccupation with the doings of the devil and his minions is combined with grim realism; there is a thin line between reality and fantasy. A hundred years later two other Spaniards, Dali and Picasso, were to express themselves in a similar way in a similar situation; civil war.

These, then, were some of the constituents of the Romantic Response. There were heroes, villains, monsters, crusades, pilgrimages, poets, and peasants, odes to Grecian Urns and Nightingales, and a generation gap. Romanticism is both rejection and escape. It is the product of inconsistency and dissonance. It looks both forward and backward in time, time which softens or gilds the ugly contours of the present. It is a state of consciousness in search of a style or form which will support or be supported by an ethos which has not yet clearly evolved. From time to time realism peeps through and anchors one's perceptions in the sordid present: we have such people as Goya, Daumier, and Dickens, but then we slip back into a world of knights in shining armor, gypsy camps, and bucolic country scenes where beautiful barefooted maidens, on a summer day, would rake the meadow sweet with hay. Rural poverty is much easier to romanticize than the ugly squalor of a city slum.

And so one may ask: when did the romantic movement come to an end? A *style* like baroque or rococo seems to have a beginning and an end, but a *movement* is a different sort of response, even though it is made to similar stimulus conditions. Perhaps if we invoke the notion of response generalization we can discern something of this sort going on today.

REFERENCES

1. Byron, G. G., Lord. *The Isles of Greece. The Standard Book of British and American Verse. Op. cit.* pp. 352-355.
2. Byron, G. G., Lord. *Childe Harold's Pilgrimage.* Canto I, VIII: 10. *Byron, Poetical Works.* Oxford University Press, 1945. p. 183.
3. Berlioz, H., Explanatory preface to "Symphony Fantastique." From record jacket ML 4467, Columbia Records.
4. Berlioz, H. *Ibid.*
5. Gautier, T. *Encycl. Brit. Op. cit.,* Vol. 3, p. 27.
6. Coleridge, S. T., *Kubla Khan. Coleridge: Poetry and Prose.* Carlos Baker (Ed.). Bantam Books, R. C. 281, 1965. p. 64.
7. Coleridge, S. T. *The Rhime of the Ancient Mariner. Op. cit.* pp. 28, 31.
8. Huxley, A., *The Complete Etchings of Goya.* Crown Publishers, 1943. p. 11.

CHAPTER XIII

Pax Europa

The dream of reason had produced monsters which were inconsistent with the dream. Was Napoleon the betrayer or fulfiller of the revolution? Could a "good thing" like the unification of Italy offset a "bad thing" like the massacres in Spain? Were the blood baths of Austerlitz (1805) and Jena (1806) and the long horrible retreat from Moscow (1812) really worth it? The avowed goal was so very reasonable— that all men should have equal opportunity, an equal standing before a universal, codified law, and all of the other benefits promised by the revolution.

But somehow this was not working out. In 1815 desperate efforts were made at the Congress of Vienna to restore the *status quo* and quench the fires of liberty. The Bourbons were restored in France, other "legitimate" governments were re-established, and an attempt was made to bring about a balance of power in which no nation could dominate Europe. National boundaries were created with no reference to the desires and needs of the populations involved. Catholic Belgium was united to Protestant Holland. Norway was taken from Denmark and given to Sweden. Italy was taken apart once more and the confederation of the Rhine broken up. One is reminded of today's condition where Germany is divided into East and West purely in the interests of an international balance of power.

But there was no European war from 1815 to 1914. This is not to say that there were not wars in Europe, but they tended to be local affairs. The Crimean war (1854) with its

"Charge of the Light Brigade" was fought on the very out-
skirts of the continent. Prussia attacked Denmark (1864) with
Austria as her ally, then turned around and attacked Austria
(1866); next France attacked Prussia and was soundly beaten
(1870). Russia went through periodic wars with Turkey and
finally marched off into the Far East to be soundly beaten by
Japan. There were wars among the Balkan states. But there
was no *European* war until *The Guns of August* began to
boom.[1]

There were also revolutions but they never seemed to get
very far. In 1830 Poland made an unsuccessful bid for independence. In France the reactionary Charles X was replaced
by Louis Philippe (the "citizen" king) with little bloodshed.
Eighteen forty-eight was a much more significant year when
Louis Philippe, with his green umbrella and stovepipe hat,
was sent packing and a republic was proclaimed; there was
severe and bloody fighting in Paris. That year the streets of
Vienna also ran with blood as students took over the city;
rioting against the Establishment is not a phenomenon unique
to our contemporary generation. There was a civil war in
Ireland and a revolt in Hungary. None of this activity accom-
plished much.

The revolution of 1848 in France produced a curious result.
The first president of the new republic was none other than
Louis Napoleon, the nephew of the great Napoleon. The election was a reasonably fair one, and Napoleon the Less won
over his left-wing competitor by a smashing five to one majority, clearly a landslide if there ever was one. That something beside republicanism was in the air is shown by the fact
that eight years previously, in 1840, the body of the great
Napoleon had been brought back from St. Helena. This had
been a day of national rejoicing and hysteria as the relics of
a Hero, a Saint, a latter day SON OF MAN returned to the
HOLY SOIL of France to be entombed in Les Invalides.

In 1852 Louis Napoleon moved from the president's office
to the throne of his uncle as Napoleon III (the designation
third was to maintain the fiction of continuity, Napoleon I's
son, an unhappy young man brought up by his mother at the

Austrian court, died at the age of twenty-one in 1832. The Bonapartists considered him to have been Napoleon II. He was taken from France when he was three years old and never returned). Now, at mid-century, it seemed that finally the time of trouble was over. The discontented minority had been put firmly in its place, there was full employment, bread was cheap, holidays and festivals were frequent, the court was brilliant, the new Empress was the most beautiful woman in Europe, and all things were being done in GOOD ORDER. Presently, squads of workmen (well paid) arrived in Paris to build the boulevards, create parks, and erect the Opera. Gounod wrote *Faust,* Offenbach wrote *Orpheus in the Underworld* with its can-can dances, Manet painted *Luncheon on the Grass,* and de Lesseps dug the Suez Canal. The political honeymoon did not last long however, and during the last ten years of its life the *regime* was beset by continuous discord and contention. Finally, the year before the disastrous Franco-Prussian war which forced his abdication, the Emperor, a tired, sick old man, called for a plebicite in an effort to find out what the people really wanted. The voices of political parties and militant minorities were so loud that perhaps the voice of the people, (silent majority?) could not be heard. He was supported by a smashing majority of five to one, the same majority that had voted him in twenty-two years previously. Apparently, the people liked their Emperor; he had given them national pride, bread, circuses, and security. He had been to Paris what Lorenzo de'Medici had been to Florence. The reason for his not being regarded as a Hero is that he did not die at the right time; instead of being killed in action against the invading barbarians he was captured and ultimately found his way to London where he died following surgery for a bladder stone. There is nothing romantic about a bladder stone; this is no way for a martyr or hero to die.

The Franco-Prussian war was a national disaster and it produced a response which was to become typical in Western culture. In and about Paris there was a concentration of the minority who had *not* voted for Napoleon III in the plebiscite, artisans and factory workers, writers and liberal intellectuals, people of the revolutionary tradition. Some of the more aggressive members of this population took over the city and formed a Commune, threw up barricades in the streets and took hostages. They captured the nerve center of the nation; the government records and administrative offices and sources of information and printing presses. If they had been doing this today the first thing they would have made for would be the radio and TV stations—how else can so few control so many?

Apparently the plan was to establish Communes in all the principal cities and then work from these centers out into the rural areas where the major opposition was expected. The plan failed due to lack of professionalism and leadership. There was no one quite as good as Lenin on hand to pick up the power and use if effectively. The Paris Commune lasted less than three months.

Is there any reasonable comparison between the Paris of Napoleon III and the Florence of Lorenzo de'Medici? Remember the description of Guiccardini (pp. 62-63). "The city enjoyed perfect peace, . . . the government so powerful that no one dared oppose it. The people every day delighted in shows, revelries, and other novelties; they were well fed, . . . activities flourished." Then Lorenzo died and the system fell apart. Louis Napoleon made a stupid blunder and his system fell apart. Maybe this was one of the medical accidents of history; his bladder stone was bothering him.

"The Influence of Medicine upon History" would make a good book title. In 1861 Prince Albert, the consort of Queen Victoria, died from pneumonia. This precipitated an acute depressive reaction in the Queen and she retired from public life. The system did not fall apart but continued to grow stronger over the years under the able professional leadership of such men as Disraeli, Gladstone, Palmerston, and the Earl of Derby. When Victoria was finally persuaded to appear once more in public she had become a symbol of the Empire, the personification of the State, and honorary custodian of *The Proud Tower*.[2] This system has shown remarkable lasting power. It was badly cracked by the first World War and given a staggering blow by World War II, but viable elements of it may still be discerned today.

But returning to the nineteenth century "Pax Europa." There was no general European war, however, there were many "little" wars throughout the world. Empire building wars. In 1840 and again in 1855 England went to war against China. Hong Kong became one of the jewels in the Imperial Crown. Mexico was invaded by the United States in 1846 and again in 1863 by France (another one of Napoleon III's blunders). However, WE did get something out of it; bits of land like Texas, Arizona, New Mexico, and California. Queen Victoria became Empress of India in 1877. There was a general land-grab in Africa. In one of these wars, England versus the Zulu tribe in 1879, the natives showed an unusual degree of punch; they sneaked up and almost eliminated a British army. Imagine the consternation and chagrin back home when the news arrived that *over eight hundred* Europeans had been killed by blacks. The episode was referred to as a massacre rather than a battle. A curious little detail about this war was the fact that Napoleon III's only son and heir, an engaging young man known as the "Prince Imperial," left his exile in England to go as a volunteer with the British army. One day while on a reconnaissance mission he was killed. The father had died from surgery, now the son was picked off by a stray bullet in darkest Africa. Not good material for Martyr and Hero legends.

Only three years before this, during the course of our own empire building operations, an American force under General George Custer had been wiped out by Indians who had resented and resisted. But Westward the course of Empire continued to find its way. By 1893 American sugar interests were able to take over the Hawaiian Islands, which had been an independent native monarchy, and in 1898 we fought the Battle of Manila Bay in which the Spanish fleet was sunk without being able to fire a shot. It sounds almost like a massacre, except this time it was white men fighting against white men for the possession of some foreign shore upon which brown men made their homes.

Around the base of the Statue of Liberty one may read these words:

> Give me your tired, your poor,
> Your huddled masses yearning to breathe free,
> The wretched refuse of your teeming shore,
> Send these, the homeless, tempest-tossed, to me:
> I lift my lamp beside the golden door.[3]
> . . .

The golden door opened into Ellis Island, teeming with immigrants, and from there the tired poor, who had just completed a tempest-tossed crossing of the Atlantic, huddled in the steerage, would move on and breathe the air of a railroad flat in New York. It would be stretching a point to say that their diet consisted of wretched refuse. The point is that there was dissonance between the ideals of liberty and the facts of economic slavery. America was a land of opportunity unless you were a native (i.e., Indian). There was a golden door through which Irish families could enter Boston (well, anyway it was gilded) but the doors to Philadelphia and Chicago had no gilt on them whatsoever for the Negro families moving up from the deep South.

The idea of nationalism was dissonant with the facts of colonialism; the ideals of a proletariat revolution clashed with the fact of an upper class establishment; it was becoming harder to romanticize rural poverty and to regard "natives" as simple dwellers in some island paradise. There was an increasing focus on the squalor of the slums. To what extent did the novels of Charles Dickens influence social reform?

The world was also getting smaller and it was easier to get about. News coverage was quicker and more complete. The crossing of the Alps by Hannibal and Napoleon were events separated in time by two thousand years, both expeditions took about two weeks, transportation had not improved significantly. However, by 1850 railroads linked all of the principal European cities and travel time had been cut by one-tenth or more. This was a revolutionary break-through. The Iron Horse was also useful in war. In 1861, 10,000 Confederate troops were moved by rail from the Shenandoah valley to Manassas Junction to tip the scales in the first battle of Bull Run.

The nineteenth century produced such changes in technology and acceleration in the tempo of life that there was hardly time to develop a *style* in the sense that Baroque was a style. We find much adaptation and borrowing. There was neo-Gothic, neo-oriental, neo-classical, neo this and neo that. The Royal Pavilion at Brighton (pleasure dome?) is a mishmash of oriental motifs. (Plate No. 41) The Houses of Parliament, designed in 1835, are a composite of Gothic forms. (Plate No. 42) In our country we have "Erie Railroad Station Gothic" while Jefferson's Monticello is neo-classic.

Innovations made their appearance but they did not create a style. The vast Crystal Palace exhibition hall in London (1851) used acres of glass held in place by an iron framework, but it would be many a year before this technique would be used for a private home. Even today most people seem to prefer neo-colonial or neo-ranch houses with the only concession to glass being a "picture window" which looks out onto the street.

Security is imparted by that which is familiar, and "neo" anything carries the aura of the tried and true. A reproduction of anything is completely safe and if an exact copy is not available the next best thing is to live with things which imitate or derive from that which is safe. Renoir reminds one of Rubens; opulent, rosy-cheeked females dance, bathe, and desport themselves in a non-controversial setting. For example, his *Moulin de la Galette* (Plate No. 43), or *Dance at Bougival* (Plate No. 44) are non-demanding; we are not required to thing of executions, slum conlitions, mystical religious experiences, or heroic exploits. We are looking at people who might have stepped out of the second act of *La Boheme*. Degas painted ballet girls, Manet did the nude *Olympia* in 1863 (Plate No. 45) which is strongly reminiscent of Titan's *Venus of Urbino* done in 1538 (Plate No. 46).

A certain type of abstraction will also induce a pleasantly

131

relaxing revery. Turner leaves out details and dissolves much of his composition into rain, steam, clouds, and mist. It is as though we were viewing a scene through half-closed eyes. Monet carries the process to its logical conclusion as he paints air and light. In his studies of the Rouen Cathedral which now hang in the Boston Museum of Fine Arts we can see a Gothic facade dissolve into nothing more than an impression, a ghostly memory trace. (Plate No. 47)

Cezanne is enchanted with Mount Sainte-Victoire, and over the years in successive paintings we see him reducing it to areas of color which give one the suggestion of a distant mountain.

Dancers, bathers, meadows, and mountains are such pleasant things, particularly when seen softly in a mysterious light; sort of like the *Purkinje shift* at nightfall.

But impressionism was only a passing fancy; it led on to *post* impressionism and then cubism. The nineteenth century produced many words beginning with *pre, post,* and *neo* and ending with *ism.* It generated many stylizations but no style in the older sense of the word. People were too busy and there were too many inconsistencies among the various elements of the cognitive structure of Western culture. Things were moving so fast that there was no time to establish a pattern for the reduction of dissonance. Marx and Engels offered solutions which were as divergent from the proposals of Bismark and Disraeli as the programs of Machiavelli had been from those of Luther.

Occasionally the arts would produce wild men, the Fauvists in France and, just before the first World War, the wildest man of all in the person of Igor Stravinski. The first performance of *The Rite of Spring* in 1913 was greeted by a full scale riot. People actually stood up in their chairs and punched each other. All kinds of dissonance is motivating. "Pax Europa" is about to come to an end.

REFERENCES

1. Tuchman, Barbara, *The Guns of August*. Macmillan, 1962.
2. Tuchman, Barbara, *The Proud Tower*. Macmillan, 1966.
3. Lazarus, Emma, part of the sonnet "The New Colossus," inscribed about the base of the Statue of Liberty.

CHAPTER XIV

The Coming of the Barbarians

Shortly before his death on the Western Front in 1915 Rupert Brooke wrote *The Soldier*:

If I should die, think only this of me:
    That there's some corner of a foreign field
That is forever England. There shall be
    In that rich earth a richer dust concealed;
A dust whom England bore, shaped, made aware,
    Gave, once, her flowers to love, her ways to roam,
A body of England's, breathing English air,
    Washed by the rivers, blest by suns of home.
And think, this heart, all evil shed away,
    A pulse in the eternal mind, no less
        Gives somewhere back the thoughts by England given;
Her sights and sounds; dreams happy as her day;
    And laughter, learnt of friends; and gentleness,
        In hearts at peace, under an English heaven.[1]

Moving ahead twenty-five years to September 1, 1939, the day the Germans invaded Poland, we find another poet, W. H. Auden, writing:

I sit in one of the dives
On Fifty-second Street
Uncertain and afraid
As the clever hopes expire
Of a low dishonest decade:

Waves of anger and fear
Circulate over the bright
And darkened lands of the earth,
Obsessing our private lives;
The unmentionable odor of death
Offends the September night.
. . .

All I have is a voice
To undo the folded lie,
The romantic lie in the brain
Of the sensual man-in-the-street
And the lie of Authority
Whose buildings grope the sky:
There is no such thing as the State
And no one exists alone;
Hunger allows no choice
To the citizens or the police;
We must love one another or die.[2]
. . .

In the *Saturday Review* issue of February 14, 1970 (p.
31) there is a poem written by a returned Vietnam veteran;
he chooses to remain anonymous:

I have been a soldier, killer, unjustified
    murderer of yellow people.
I have been to the center of my life
where the animal lives
and rivers run red with blood.

to this night, to you.
I have come home now,
to the night I have come, through the
    village of dead children.
through hell

listen to me church,
listen to me friends of the church,
if we are not moved by Songmy
nothing will move us.
and not even God will save us from
hell.[3]

136

Brooke, the soldier, is morbidly preoccupied with premonitions of his own death. He has a sentimental attachment to home, to the flowers, streams, byways, and hedges of England. He is sad but not mad. He is completely centered about his own emotions.

Twenty-five years later Auden is uncertain and afraid, angry and disillusioned. There is no such thing as the State, as a mystical entity called America or England or Germany or Poland. Auden is not self-centered; no one lives alone and we must love each other or die.

But we have not loved each other and people are dying. The anonymous soldier today is so very different from Brooke's plaintive melancholy fellow who dreams of returning home to gentleness and hearts at peace. This young soldier has come home to darkness through a village of dead children. Western civilization has come a long way from Kipling's "Barrack room ballads." ("But when it comes to slaughter, you will do your work on water.")[4]

Rupert Brooke's England was the England of Kipling, of the Empire upon which the sun never set, of the white man's burden, of the playing fields of Eaton and Harrow, of leisurely weekends at country homes, and of a well-trained servant class. If one bothered to inquire, one might discover that the second assistant parlor maid's nephew was an orphaned ragamuffin sleeping in the gutters of London. But this would create dissonance, so we had best not know about it. Bread was not cheap, but there were some entertainments. A scant four years before the end of *Pax Europa* Edward VII died and London was treated to the spectacle of the most stupendous funeral procession of all time; it was loaded with crowned heads; emperors, kings, princes, sultans, emirs, rajas, grand dukes, little dukes, and archbishops. There were also horses and liveried grooms.

Today there are hardly any crowned heads left and grooms as a class are extinct. So are parlor maids. Today public relief and aid to dependent children pays better. Today there are hardly any ragamuffins sleeping in the gutters of London and New York; there are none at all in Stockholm and Copenhagen; but there are many in Calcutta and Bombay.

Today the world has become so small that it takes less time to fly from London to Calcutta than it did to take the train (first class) from one's Highland hunting lodge to London, or the Fall River Line from Newport, Rhode Island to New York. O, for the romance and glamour of those good old days when paddle-wheel steamers wound their way up the East River every evening.

But for better or for worse those good old days are gone forever. Today the American Empire is the universal state of Western Culture in the same way that Rome was the universal state of Greek culture. We are big, very big, and our frontiers extend to the uttermost parts of the earth. Yet, no matter how far out we go, whatever frontier we choose, it will be closer to home than, say, the North of England was to Hadrian or the Danube frontier was to Marcus Aurelius. The Roman empire was bigger on a time-distance continuum than we ever possibly could become. The only logical limit is the entire world. England has cast her mantle upon us; now what are we going to do about it?

This, then, is the stage upon which we, as psychologists, are looking at Western Culture. We see the heartland of our own traditions and values. Long week-ends in the country, labor-saving devices, good roads, fast cars, and a man on the moon. We also see, if we care or dare to look, waste, pollution, discrimination, dissatisfaction, and dissonance. Our own sizable internal proletariat does not seem to be satisfied. What's wrong with our bread and circuses? Why doesn't somebody do something about it? Why can't we get that nasty little copper filling out of our quarters? Why isn't it safe to walk the city streets at night? Today Mr. Auden would never get as far as the dive on Fifty-second Street; he would be mugged before he got there!

And we do have a nasty little war going on at the frontier. Hadrian's wall has been breeched and the external proletariat, the barbarians, are being *extremely* stubborn. It's even worse than the Zulu war in which the Prince Imperial was killed.

The casualty lists make us sad and make some of us mad, but after all, there are as many of our boys killed over a holiday week-end in fast cars as are killed in that little old frontier war in maybe two or three weeks. This thought *should* be a handy way to reduce dissonance, but somehow it doesn't seem to.

It is so much fun to read history and day-dream about what *might* have been if a critical situation had been resolved differently. What would have happened if Lee had won the battle of Gettysburg, which he *almost* did. What would have been the outcome if England had decided to intervene on the side of the South, she *almost* did. *If* that had happened there might have been a British army backing up Lee at Gettysburg and a British fleet at New Orleans to keep the Mississippi open so that cotton would continue to flow into the power looms of England. This *almost* happened.

Can you hear a debate in Parliament? The Prime Minister is on the spot; why are so many English boys dying in America? The P.M. explains his new policy; it is *Confederatization* of the war; we are now training and equipping the Southern armies, and just as soon as they are able to take over the major responsibility for the independence of the Confederacy, we will pull out. We have set up a time-table for this, but if the North continues to infiltrate it will slow the process down. For example, at the present time Sherman is marching through Georgia from Atlanta to the sea cutting a path of devastation, so we have not been able to bring any troops home this month. When pressed the P.M. admitted that little progress was being made at the Paris peace talks. Boos from the back bench.

This bit of fantasy is completely ridiculous, but it is fun to read history and wonder about what might have been. Was there any way in which the Dark Ages could have been prevented? What could have been done then to prevent the death of the ancient world? It had so many good things and the dark ages were so terribly dark.

Well—just suppose, just suppose, mind you, that at some point in the history of the decline and fall of the Roman empire there had been a group of intellectuals in power who realized that, in fact, the Empire was declining. You can't do anything about anything until you realize that something needs to be done. Now suppose, just suppose, that the decision was made to leave Britain to the British, Jerusalem to the Jews, Egypt to the Egyptians, Syria to the Syrians and so forth. That their problems were their problems; that Rome would draw back to Rome and create a model state comprising nothing more than, say, the Italian peninsula, and within this state everything would be done in perfect order; it would be so good that the rest of the world would want to imitate it; it would become the storehouse of values; the repository of culture; the place where people would come from all over the world to study and learn.

Suppose that they also decided that slavery, as an institution, must be abolished, that the small independent farmer must return to his farm, that free grain must no longer be imported from Egypt, and that feeding Christians to the lions in the Coliseum was not an edifying activity.

Under these circumstances the barbarians might not have gotten closer than the Alps unless they came as students, and there might have been a very large enrollment of foreigners at the baths (universities) of Rome. Under these circumstances Rome might not have fallen and the universal state of Greek culture would have been immortal.

In order for a system to perpetuate itself we have postulated that dissonance must be at an optimal level; neither too high to disrupt nor so low that stagnation results. This implies a reasonable congruence between belief and action; between what people say and what they do. Thus it is inconsistent for an autocracy to govern behind a facade of republican forms; a feudal system may be obnoxious to many, but it has a certain element of honesty, we call a spade a spade. It is inconsistent to talk about liberty, freedom, equality, and so on when, in fact, they do not exist; we must either "tell it like it is" or change it so that it is like we tell it.

If we postulate that a certain level of achievement motivation is necessary for the health and vigor of a society, then there must exist in that society conditions which make achievement possible. There must be patrons of the arts and reinforcements for creative activity. If we postulate that the need for achievement is a mild form of aggression, aggression which has been sublimated into useful activity, then there must be a moderate level of frustration, not high enough to produce overt acts of hostility or so low that all challenge goes out of life. The conditions of existence must be neither too hard nor too soft. If everything is free, why bother to work; if, no matter how hard you work, you don't get anywhere, you are likely to join the revolution.

Under such circumstances one would expect a minimum number of people making the SON-OF-MAN or the ANTI-SATAN responses. There would be little mannerism and very few etchings like Goya's *Disasters of the War*. We might expect more productions like Botticelli's *Birth of Venus,* and from the hands of less gifted artists, perhaps some rather trite material. One might expect a shift toward the "Humanities" and abstract mathematics.

Guicciardini's description of Florence—"The city enjoyed perfect peace . . ." and so on (pp. 62-63, read it again) seems to fit all of the conditions listed above; but then Lorenzo died. We then had Savanorola, the Borgia family, and the age of Machiavelli. How could this have been prevented? One answer would be to have had someone as capable as Lorenzo, *not* his son, ready to continue in charge of things. Is this the major independent variable with which we have to contend?

Now taking a peek into the future with the aid of our Ouija board and a clouded crystal ball, we can make the guarded prediction that we are standing at the brink of another attack of DARK AGES. All of the signs point in this direction. We can solace ourselves with the thought that things move so rapidly today that they probably will not last for five hundred years this time, perhaps only a generation or two, but this is scant comfort for those of us who are past the first flush of youth.

For those who refuse to admit that a culture is not immortal, and desire to impose some sort of immortality upon our own, the following program is suggested:

First, pull the Empire back to the smallest size which is compatible with natural boundaries, an area within which we could follow Rousseau's advice that "the land should suffice for the maintenance of the inhabitants, and that there should be as many inhabitants as the land can maintain."

Second, in order to expedite the first proposal, almost all scientific enterprise must be directed at population control and food production. Ecology will be the queen of the sciences.

Third, we must get rid of the notion that because a person can win an election he is therefore a good administrator. The business of government will be in the hands of highly trained professionals; an extension of the town manager type of government. Everyone could vote but not everyone would be eligible to run for office. Thus, when someone like Lorenzo d'Medici died or retired his successor would be hired from a (small?) panel of eligible experts. Issues of general public concern like the legalization of this or the prohibition of that would be determined by plebicite without reference to parties or personalities. The game of politics as we have understood it will become a thing of the past.

Fourth, order, in certain areas, will become an absolute rather than a relative matter. It will be as much of an absolute as aseptic technique is in an operating room, and for the same reason, patients die of infection.

Now to continue our medical analogy, pathogenic bacteria in a social sense are the disadvantaged and frustrated who create disorder, so clearly the analogy here is with public health. We control the conditions which produce infection. This brings us to our fifth and last point.

Bread (welfare) and circuses (television) are not enough. Subsumed under Ecology there must be a program designed to keep frustration and dissonance within certain limits. Something completely different from our present notions of the Welfare State. As psychologists we will think in terms of two simple definitions, that "frustration comes from the thwarting of ongoing motivated behavior" and dissonance from "inconsistencies among the various elements of the cognitive structure." Now it seems rather simple—all we have to do is to not thwart people *when they are motivated* to do something useful and in all things to call a spade a spade, that is, to avoid inconsistencies. The crystal ball is still clouded with respect to unmotivated people. Perhaps they will have to become grooms and washer-women. No question about it, our service personnel, from the porter to the parlor maid, are in short supply.

Students of Japanese history will recognize that a situation roughly like that described above existed for two hundred and fifty years during the Tokugawa Period from 1600 to 1850. It served to perpetuate the culture and avoid a dark age.

Now if we wish to try this, or something like it, we should be able to read some of the signs of the times so that we can know where we stand at any particular moment. This is feedback. In order to be consistent with the rest of the book we will look, for the last time, at a few more paintings.

It has been pointed that Guiccardini's conditions of good order in a small state did produce a radiantly beautiful thing like Botticelli's *Birth of Venus*. Now look at a painting done in 1880 in Germany during the well-ordered rule of Bismark; Bocklin's *The Isle of the Dead*. It is serene, slightly depressing, and has a certain melancholy beauty. (Plate No. 48)

There are no burning issues. Dissonance is neither too high nor too low. This may be taken as a sign that everything is going along pretty well.

In England in 1865 Disraeli and the Earl of Derby had things fairly well under control and Rosetti painted *The Bride*. Comment is superfluous. (Plate No. 49)

In 1890 a Swiss painter named Ferdinand Hodler did *The Night*. It would seem we have no cause for concern. (Plate No. 50)

In the presence of this sort of cultural product or a mild form of abstraction such as impressionism or music by a Wagner or a Tchaikovsky we can feel reasonably sure that there is no immediate danger.

But now if we move up to 1914 and look at de Chirico's

Melancholy and Mystery of a Street we are vaguely disquieted. There is something threatening out there. This painting has some of the melancholy seen in Bocklin's *Isle of the Dead,* and it is of interest to note that de Chirico studied Bocklin while he was an art student, but the pupil has introduced a feeling of anxiety, foreboding, and dread. He has gone mannerist on us. (Plate No. 51)

Look at the distortion and exaggeration of perspective. Where is that poor little girl going with her hoop, and WHAT ON EARTH could be casting that shadow we see in the middle distance? You may look upon this cultural product as a possible symptom of illness in the *status quo.*

At last we come to the period of World War II with Tchelitchew's *Hide-and-Seek,* which hangs in the Museum of Modern Art in New York. There is a little girl in this picture too, perhaps this is where de Chirico's little girl got to when she reached the end of the street. (Plate No. 52)

John Canady says of this: "In a wondrous tangle of membranes, blood vessels, plant forms, bodies, and suggestions of internal organs, we are led in and out of recognizability as one image merges with or is transformed into another. *Hide-and-Seek* is a section through the cancer of an anguished world where agony of spirit cannot be assuaged but must be compulsively probed."[5]

This may be one of the symptoms of the terminal illness of Western culture. This is not amusing, we have gone far beyond the moustache on the Mona Lisa.

REFERENCES

1. Brooke, R. *The Soldier. The Standard Book of British and American Verse. Op. cit.* p. 729.
2. Auden, W. H. *September 1, 1939. Immortal Poems of the English Language. Op. cit.* p. 583.
3. Anon. *The Saturday Review,* Feb. 14, 1970. p. 31.
4. Kipling, R. *Barrack Room Ballads,* "Gunga Din."
5. Canaday, J. *Mainstreams of Modern Art.* Holt, Rinehart and Winston, 1959. p. 542.

Index

Huxley, Aldous, 121

Ignatius of Antioch, Saint, 7, 8, 18, 21, 23, 24
Immaculate Conception, 13
indulgence, 74
industrial revolution, 108
Isaiah, O. T. book of—, 19

Jackson, "Stonewall," 18
Jefferson, Thomas, 58, 109, 131
Jehovah's Witnesses, 31
Jerome, Saint, 27, 28
Jerusalem, 4, 5, 43
Jesuit, 30, 77, 88, 89
Jesus Christ, 8, 10, 13, 19, 21, 22, 35
Jew, Jewish, 5, 6, 12, 57, 140
John, Saint, 10, 11
John III, pope, 40
Johnson, Dr. Samuel, 106
Joseph of Arimathea, 8
Josephus Flavus, 6
Judaism, 3, 13, 19, 40
Judas Maccabeus, 3
Julius II, pope, 73
Justinian, 38

Kipling, 137
Kosciusko, 115

labor force, 108
Lamb (of God), 7, 9, 14
Lear (Shakespeare), 83, 84
Lee, Robert E., 139
Lenin, 24
Leo X, pope, (Giovanni de Medici), 73, 74
Locke, John, 96, 102
loom, power, 106, 111
Louis XIV, King of France, 91, 92, 97, 99
Louis XVI, King of France, 24
Louis Philippe, King of France, 126
LSD, 10
Luke, Saint, 6, 33
Luther, Martin, 30, 71, 72, 74, 76, 88, 89

Machiavelli, 70, 71, 73, 97, 110, 141
Manet, 127, 131
Mannerism, 69, 75, 76, 77, 78, 79, 81, 92, 105
Mao Tse-tung, 23
Marco Polo, 55
Marcus Aurelius, 34, 138
Mark, Saint, 5, 7
martyr, martyrdom, 7, 8, 18, 19, 21, 23, 24, 25, 48, 129
Marx, Karl, 24, 132
Mary, the Virgin, 1, 9, 10, 11, 12, 13, 14, 22, 26, 27, 28, 44
Masaccio, 64
McClelland, D. C. (achievement motivation), 41, 46, 140
Medici, Lorenzo, "il Magnifico," 62, 63, 65, 66, 67, 69, 77, 127, 128, 141, 142
meditation, 10
Methodists, the Wesleys, 31, 111
Michelangelo, 63, 71, 77, 78, 87
Middle Ages, medieval, 48, 55, 57
Milan, edict of—, 21
Mill, John Stuart, 58, 59, 63, 102
Milton, John, 83, 84, 85, 86, 97, 116
miracle, 8, 36
Mohammed, 19, 45
Monet, 132
Mona Lisa, 1, 9, 43
monk, monasticism, 25, 28, 30, 65
monasteries, 28
(friars), 29
Mormons, Latter Day Saints, 10
Moroni, Angel, 10
mosaics, 35, 37, 39, 48

Napoleon I, 90, 115, 125, 126, 127, 130
Napoleon III, 126, 127, 128, 129
Nero, 5
Newton, Sir Isaac, Newtonian, 81, 92, 96, 99, 102, 105, 106, 111, 113
Nicea, council of—, 22
Nicholas II, Romanov, 23, 99

Odoacer, 36
Offenbach, 127
Orthodox, orthodoxy, 21, 34, 35, 43

147